Tradeshow
Success

Tradeshow Success

14 Proven Steps to Take Your Tradeshow Marketing to the Next Level

Sarah —
to your tradeshow success!
J. Patt

Timothy Patterson

Bulk Sales

Oregon Blue Rock, LLC offers excellent discounts on this book when ordered in quantity for bulk purchase.

For more information, please contact:
media@tradeshowsuccessbook.com
503-507-4110

ISBN: 0692446362
ISBN 13: 9780692446362

CONTENTS

FOREWORD

You can enroll in expensive and valuable tradeshow marketing training courses at ExhibitorLive or online and learn a ton of great, useful, and actionable information that can help you do your job better. This book isn't meant to replace them.

Hardly.

Instead, think of *Tradeshow Success* as an inspired look at more than a dozen critical areas you need to be aware of in order to succeed.

Sadly, too many tradeshow managers don't know they're missing key pieces. They wonder why their results are mediocre or why their neighbors down the aisle are packing them in, kicking ass, and taking names.

There are university-level tradeshow marketing courses that can help elevate your career. However, it's doubtful that you can find a book that will help you bootstrap your way to tradeshow marketing success quite like the specific ways this book will.

Experience and research have shown that the practices detailed in this book *will* increase awareness, attract more media coverage, bring more people to your booth, increase leads, and generate more revenue.

I'm deeply indebted to Mel White of Classic Exhibits, who has encouraged me from the moment the book was conceived through several drafts. My wife, Jenny, has been a source of inspiration and motivation and without her this book would probably still be languishing in my laptop.

So, enjoy. It's all in here, and it's all worked for countless exhibitors who came before you.

INTRODUCTION

Are you tired of throwing away hard-earned money on tradeshows? Do you wonder why some companies seem to be blessed with great results, opening new markets, finding new clients, and seeing their businesses grow year after year, whereas you're just sitting there, fuming, because the last few times you exhibited you saw a *lot* of dollars go down the drain with nothing to show for it?

Are tradeshow exhibits still a wise decision in the twenty-first century? Or maybe you are saying, "I know I can use tradeshow marketing to build my business. I'm just not sure how to do it effectively!"

If you're not seeing these results, it's not because tradeshow marketing doesn't work. It *does* work. You just haven't figured out *how* to make it work for *you*.

The first question—Are tradeshows still a wise marketing decision?—evolves from the technological explosion of the last decade, social media in particular, and its effect on traditional marketing practices. So much has been written about the new way of connecting with potential audiences that I could reference hundreds of books, blogs, speakers, authors, and more who are touting the "new media."

It seems that the question might best be reframed as, "Can tradeshow marketing, given the challenge of face-to-face connections in a digital world, still give you sufficient return on investment (ROI) to make it worthwhile?" (We'll get back to the ROI question later.)

I suggest that the evidence is here: Tradeshows can help grow your company, spread the word about your brand, and increase sales. However, just showing up at the tradeshow with a nice booth and a few staffers is no longer enough, if it ever was in the first place.

Perhaps there was a time when setting up a booth brought you traffic, visitors, and new leads. However, there's much more to it than that now.

To show that tradeshow marketing can be a very marketing effective tool, look no further than Bob's Red Mill, an Oregon company that makes hundreds of stoneground grain and related natural food products.

Bob Moore, the iconic "Bob" of Bob's Red Mill, whose likeness appears on every single product package, gives kudos to tradeshow marketing. In a 2012 interview with *Oregon Business* magazine, Bob was quoted as saying, "You can't grow outside your territory unless you go to tradeshows."

Bob's Red Mill currently occupies a 320,000 square foot facility in Milwaukie, Oregon and employs upwards of 400 people. Bob made headlines in February 2010, when, on Bob's 81st birthday, he announced that he was giving the company to his employees in an Employee Stock Ownership Plan.

Founded in 1978, Bob's Red Mill has seen steady growth for more than three decades. In the past few years, it has generated multi-million-dollar sales increases each year.

In fact, that's a multi-million-dollar story that this book tells. According to a 2010 *Inc.* article, the privately owned company's estimated annual income was estimated at "$70 million in whole-grain flours and cereals, with annual growth rates between 20 and 30 percent." The company has ramped up distributorship to the point where they're in virtually every grocery story in the US and Canada and 70 other countries. How did they do it?

Certainly, as Bob indicated, tradeshows are a large part. About a decade after its foundation, Bob's Red Mill moved into tradeshow marketing.

The company's marketing team has implemented a number of ideas detailed in this book, including:

- booth staff training
- creating attention-getting activities in their tradeshow booth (for example, hiring a Dixieland band to march through the show floor with Bob in the lead is a common occurrence)

- worked diligently in pre-show marketing and scheduling client and distributor meetings during the show
- designed and built two large custom booths in the last ten years
- worked with an outside agency, Koopman Ostbo of Portland, to handle media outreach and other services such as graphic design
- had Ken Koopman of Koopman Ostbo, write a book detailing Bob's story to use as a book-signing giveaway at tradeshows
- been active on social media

In other words, they believe in – and have invested heavily in – tradeshow marketing. They exhibit at a pair of large industry expo shows each year – Natural Products Expo West and East. In addition, they attend smaller shows throughout the year for continued outreach. They have a definite purpose for attending each show and definable objectives, whether it's a small educational show with a few hundred visitors or a large expo with thousands of attendees.

As Bob's Red Mill's 'Tradeshowguy' for over a decade, I've been involved in the process of handling virtually all of their tradeshow-related materials. I led a project team in 2005 as we designed and fabricated a custom 20x20 booth. Seven years later, shortly after starting my new company, I led another team as we designed and fabricated a 30x30 booth. A year late the booth size was increased to 30x40.

Suffice it to say, Bob's Red Mill has proven that a key element of building a company's brand awareness and reaching new markets is through steadfast and dedicated use of tradeshow marketing and outreach.

In spite of technology's vast reach and ability to digitally connect people, tradeshows still work. Face it, people still love to see each other face-to-face. They like to shake hands, laugh and smile, ask questions, and get to know the people whom they are doing, or will do, business with. As much as social media can help make those connections (and we'll cover that in the book), personal interaction with another human being trumps digital interaction every time. *Every time.*

However, exhibiting at a tradeshow means *much* more than setting up a booth, shaking hands with visitors, and showing off products or services. If it were that easy, every company would exhibit at as many tradeshows as possible.

Tradeshows are or can be expensive. It costs a lot of money to design and fabricate a booth and rent the space, not to mention adding in the costs of travel and lodging, entertaining clients, setting up the booth, and shipping it back and forth from the show. Those numbers add up. If you don't know what you're doing, you can easily come to the conclusion that tradeshows are a waste of money, because you didn't get out of them what you thought you would.

Somewhere along the way, you'll have to determine the desired return on your tradeshow investment. Your investment includes the booth, the booth space, graphic design and production, travel and lodging for staffers, salary, preshow preparation, lead generation tools, follow-up, and much more.

Are your investment dollars giving you sufficient return? For every $10,000 spent on a tradeshow, your goal is to show at least $1 in profit after expenses. That's net profit, not gross, and it must come directly from the leads generated at the show.

It's not necessarily easy, because there are lots of moving parts in determining that final figure, but it's probably easier than calculating ROI on your social media marketing.

There are many books available that outline organizational plans to do tradeshows right. In fact, when I first got into the business in 2002, I read several of them. I talked to many authors for my long-running (but since retired) podcast on tradeshow marketing. I learned a lot from those resources and from speaking to consultants, experts, and seasoned exhibitors. In the past several years, I've yet to see any new books looking into the practice of tradeshow marketing that discuss the importance of the world of social media.

Throughout this book, you'll meet both fictional and living tradeshow marketers. The real ones are here to share real-life lessons. The fictional ones are here to pose hypothetical situations and to provide longer, in-depth conversations illuminating various aspects of tradeshow marketing. Of course, we'll make sure to let you know which is which.

If you want to understand how to deconstruct your current and perhaps ineffective tradeshow marketing model and build it back up, this is the book for you.

Each step ends with a challenge for you and your marketing team. Read the step and then pull your team together to discuss the questions. Or if you want to really dig deep into the process, give them a copy of the book and spend a half-day session slicing and dicing the questions from several angles. Make sure a pool and a bar are nearby so that you can all relax after spending so much time working on your tradeshow marketing.

Whether you bring your team together for just a brief Q & A or really dig into it, know this: all of the information will be valuable to your tradeshow marketing success.

I trust you'll learn and enjoy.

———◆———

GOING WITH OR WITHOUT A MAP?

Let's say you're planning a trip. This is a trip that you've dreamed about for years. Perhaps you're driving across the country and want to stop at historical and cultural highlights. You want to visit old friends and relatives along the way.

So where do you start? Do you make a few sandwiches, pile everyone in the car, grab your wallet, make sure you have your GPS-enabled smartphone for directions, and then hit the road, hoping for the best?

I've done that. I knew where I was going, but mainly I navigated without maps and headed several hundred miles across California, knowing only the general direction I needed to go. I made a few unplanned stops along the way and the trip was a success. However, there wasn't much to it. I didn't have a huge agenda, nor did I have many expectations, other than getting there and perhaps taking in a few sights along the way. And I didn't have a lot of money on the line.

But let's say that instead of the trip being me driving solo, I had friends and family involved, and the trip was longer and more people had a say in where we were going, what we did, and how we spent the budget. And let's add that if we missed some of the stops, we'd lose all of the money. It would be clear then that we'd have to set some ground rules and plan.

Tradeshow marketing follows the same model. If you don't really plan, but instead set out with a small pop-up booth, a couple of Velcro stick-on graphics, and a clipboard with blank paper for collecting the contact information of interested visitors, you won't get much out of it. Sure, you'll "get there," and it won't cost much, so there's a low level of risk. If that's all you want, you might be happy.

But if, like our intrepid travelers, you want to come back with measurable results, you have to have a plan. In the case of the travelers, your itinerary would include the intended stops and related contact numbers. You'd need the right clothes and supplies for each stop. You'd bring along an appropriate camera with plenty of digital storage for capturing the memories. And your plan would include a detailed budget based on expenditures. That's just for starters.

In the case of a tradeshow, you'd want to ensure that you understood the playing field. It's like football, rugby, baseball, and basketball. If you don't understand the field and the rules of the game, there's no sense getting involved.

If I was asked to join a game of cricket, I'd have to take a pass. I know nothing about cricket. I've heard the term *sticky wicket*, which may or may not be connected to cricket. So, no, not me. Not now.

To understand the tradeshow game and its playing field, you'd know that they are staging grounds for branding showcases, and that three-dimensional marketing entails much more than just great graphics and a nice-looking booth. You'd understand your goals and objectives; your entire marketing staff would understand *why* you're there and *what* it means for the company. Building and enhancing the knowledge base of your employees and tradeshow marketing team is critical to your tradeshow success. Ensure that they not only understand company goals, but that they also believe in those goals. That way, all staffers from the front line, lowest paid assistant to the CEO, knows and believes in the exercise.

We'll refer to that knowledge base several times in this book. It's one of the keys to delivering stellar results. If you learn how to deliver consistently stellar results, you become the company rock star. You become valuable to any company you work for.

Creating a tradeshow marketing plan for a year is like planning a series of cruises to a dozen countries. If you don't build in as much detail into the plan as possible, a lot can go wrong. Ending up two continents away from your final destination is not a desired outcome.

Ask yourself, when you are sitting in your office the day after the big tradeshow and you find yourself saying, "That was a great show because we did_____," what answer fills that blank?

Answer that and you'll have a good idea of your real objectives. Is it two hundred fifty new leads? Is it five new distributors? Is it meeting the CEO of a company you want to do business with? Is it a screaming mob at your booth for much of the show? Whatever your answer, keep it in mind as you build your show objectives and your show plans.

Goal Setting

To help frame your tradeshow strategy for the coming year, let's meet our first fictional character, Katie, a marketing director in her late twenties.

She works for Gotcha! Cookies 'n' Treats, a company that has been in business a little more than five years. In the past three, it has been moving further into tradeshow marketing and has seen some initial success.

Katie has a steady boyfriend. They are both avid outdoorsy types and spend a lot of their free time hiking and bicycling. She's been with the company for half its life.

The company attends more than six shows a year, presenting its array of fresh-baked cookies, scones, and other treats. Visitors literally eat them up, and the company has added several new distributors, which has led to growing pains.

At this point, Katie isn't sure of how much the company will grow, or even if she wants to stick around for another two or three years. Still, she believes in the company.

The company has a relatively new 10' x 10' booth, a showstopper with large, catchy graphics. The backdrop is an image of a large cookie with a big bite gone. Visitors have told them it makes their mouth water.

The booth includes two small sample tables and a couple of equally small storage counters. Given the limited booth size and the large, attractive back wall, the company doesn't have a true table in the booth. However, management realizes that having a small meeting table will come in handy. So an expansion to a 10' x 20' booth is under discussion.

When it comes to tradeshow goal setting for Gotcha! Cookies 'n' Treats, here's where I'd start with Katie:

1. What is your main show objective?
2. What is your secondary objective?
3. Who in your company defines those goals and objectives?
4. How well are you currently meeting those goals, and how do you track them?
5. Understanding that each tradeshow has a different target market and different set of attendees, how do your goals and objectives change from show to show?
6. What is your target audience?
7. Do the shows you exhibit at meet that target?
8. Who are your main competitors?
9. How do those competitors stack up against you in terms of the following:
    a. Booth size and scope
    b. Presence (show sponsorship or other advertising opportunities)
    c. Staffing
    d. Preshow marketing
    e. Market and branding visibility

While it is useful for Katie to answer these questions, a second, ultimately more useful step, would be to address the questions with other members of the management team. The more members of her marketing and management team who chime in, the more in-depth the answers and the more common understanding the team as a whole will arrive at.

Why should all members of the team address these questions, and not just the marketing director, the owner, CEO, and so forth? Because when it comes to tradeshow marketing, research has shown that the deeper the knowledge base of the company, the more the overall success.

It's critical to increase a company's *knowledge base* (there's that term again!). Spreading such knowledge throughout the company is important, as it will come into play during the planning and execution of tradeshows.

A booth staffer may receive a question at a show that is out of the realm of her expertise, and if she is ill informed about the company's products and services, she might not have an appropriate answer. At the very least, she should know enough to refer that question to the right person. At the very best, she knows the answer, which will impress the visitor, saving time and energy for other queries. With her increased knowledge, she is more valuable to the company.

Imagine Katie and I having the following conversation about her company's goals:

"What is your most important takeaway from this show? Are you looking for more distributors, more orders? Do you just want to make sure that your current distributors are well taken care of?"

"Oh, definitely, more distributors," said Katie. "While we want to make sure that our current sellers are happy, we are in an expansion mode and are looking for more distribution. Most of them would be in the western half of the United States. Expanding nationwide is something we're looking at long term."

"OK," I said. "That sounds good. What would be your second objective?"

"We'd want everyone to know about our new line of walnut cookies. They're just off the line, and we have high hopes for them," said Katie.

"That's good. Who in the company defines the show objectives? Now, I'm not referring to the overall goals and objectives in your tradeshow marketing, but your specific goals for this specific show."

"It's essentially Debbie—the owner—and me. We'll talk it over with our bakers and our branding agency, but really, it boils down to Debbie and me."

"Excellent! How well do you meet those goals in your tradeshow marketing?"

"Hmm, that's a good question. I suspect we do OK, but I think we can do a better job of tracking it."

"It?" I asked.

"How many leads we get and whether they're increasing from year to year, show to show. I mean, we do track all of that information, somewhere." She paused. "I'm just not sure where all the information is kept from the past couple of years."

"No one has built a spreadsheet, for instance, to show the number of leads from year to year, show to show, which lists new clients, including sales?" I was thinking of a good customer relationship management (CRM) tool, with an automated follow-up.

"Not in great detail. We have overall quarterly figures and certainly know how our sales do year to year, but show to show…no. We don't break it down that much," said Katie.

"OK, let's leave that for another time. What about this? Understanding that each tradeshow has a different target audience and mix of attendees, how do your goals and objectives change from show to show?"

"That's easy," she replied. "We do the same seven shows a year. While most are to show our products and have people sample them, there are two shows that are different: they're local shows where we are strictly looking for sales. We don't see potential distributors there, but they're good sales for us, and they help to spread the gospel of Gotcha! Cookies 'n' Treats and let local people know which stores carry them."

"So there's a distinct difference between the two types of shows?"

"Yes."

"What about the other, nonlocal shows?" I asked.

"Those are to reach a wider target. They're either multistate or they're nationwide. They work pretty well for that. We hand out thousands of samples, talk to dozens of potential distributors, and continue to get in front of people with our brand and logo."

"What about PR? Do you target industry or mainstream media to entice them to do features on the company?"

"We've stumbled into it a few times. Admittedly, we could do a better job of that. I suspect that if we spent time prior to the show lining up interviews, we would get better results. But we're not skilled at that."

"Understood. It often takes an agency that is familiar with the industry and has the media contacts to make that happen. Of course, you pay the agency to make it happen, but it can often mean making impressions in front of millions of people.

"OK, Katie, let's move on. What about your target audience? How would you describe your ideal target audience?"

"Do you mean in terms of customers who eat our products, or which distributors would carry the products in their stores?"

"Let's start with the products themselves."

"OK. Well, naturally, anyone who likes sweet treats, cookies, and yummy fresh-baked snacks. We also feature a line of gluten-free cookies—"

"Because that market is exploding," I interrupted.

"Absolutely. Plus, they help you stand out a bit. Not a lot, because so many people are doing it. But it shows that you're responding to the market."

"What about distributors? What kinds of stores are you looking for?"

"It's probably easier to tell you what we're not looking for. We don't have the capacity to do fulfillment for Wal-Mart or Target, for instance. But we could take on regions for Whole Foods or Kroger, as well as the smaller chains. And while we can certainly ship across the country quickly, we tend to focus on stores in the western United States."

"Does this show meet that target?"

"Yes. All shows that we exhibit at meet that target."

"Good. Now, which companies are your main competitors at these shows? And I mean at all shows, not just the big one or two national shows that we've been discussing."

Katie paused and scrunched her face.

"That's a question we haven't really spent a lot of time on. We figure if we take care of our own product, we'll do OK."

"Can you name any competitors?" I asked.

"Sure. There's Yum's Fresh Baked Goods, Jenny's Baking, and 20-20 Cookies. Beyond that, there are a few others, but I suppose those are the main ones."

"So here's the bonus question, Katie: what do you know about those companies? In particular, what new can you find out about them by visiting their booths at the shows?"

"I do know a lot about their products. I've seen them in stores. But I admit that we were understaffed at the show, so we didn't have time to explore for more than a few minutes before and after the hall closed. But I see what you're getting at. It would be good to see their new products and see what kind of booth they have."

"And it would be helpful to determine if their branding matches their image, among other things," I explained. "Not to mention, how do they compare to you. Check their booth size, and look for things such as show sponsorships or other in-show advertising, staffing level at the booth, and whether the staff seems well trained and attentive. Understand how they compare to you in terms of market and branding visibility.

"All of these things are important," I continued, "because they show the company's full tradeshow threat. Are they really in full battle mode or are they just showing up and going through the motions?"

Katie didn't respond because she was busy making notes in her book. When she finally came up for air, she smiled and said, "It would seem to me that there's more work to be done."

There's always more work to be done. If you're not the best among your competitors, it'll take work to get there. If you're the best, it'll take even more work to stay there. So yes, there's always work to be done. And even if you don't want or need to be at the top of the market, you still want to pay your employees, stay solvent, sell product, and perhaps develop new products. Yes, there's always work to be done.

So let's recap.

Much of your marketing strategy comes down to understanding the forces in the marketplace and those that affect your company.

There is a much-taught model called the SWOT Analysis:

Strengths
Weaknesses
Opportunities
Threats

As business and marketing strategist Tony Marino said in a 2014 blog post on TrinityWebWorks.com, "In many respects, the SWOT Analysis is a report card on where a company is positioned in the competitive marketplace. Any attempt to identify the direction a company should take in the future must be grounded in an honest understanding of where that company is now."

Books have been written about the SWOT Analysis, and college professors have advanced their careers by teaching the intricacies of it. We're not going to dig that deep. So let's just say this: The better you know your company's advantages and disadvantages and how the marketplace (and other forces) can affect it, the better prepared you'll be to craft a strategy to move forward with a greater chance of success.

I would wager that very few companies go through the process of the SWOT Analysis, because the process, if done correctly, is time consuming. However, every company should understand its strengths and weaknesses regarding tradeshow marketing.

Most small to medium companies take a more pragmatic approach to their tradeshow marketing: spend a little for a bare-bones booth, show up, and kick ass. Of course, that doesn't happen without careful planning.

Others say, "We don't care what it takes. We know that by dominating our competitors at the biggest shows in our industry, we will come away with much more than we had before."

The first statement comes from a belief that "We'd better do something, because we've been told that tradeshow marketing can help us. But we've also heard that it can be a big waste of money."

The second viewpoint is more succinct: "Tradeshow marketing is the best thing we can do to reach new markets and maintain our position in the marketplace."

Company One is hedging its bets. Company Two is laying it all on the table, knowing it has a winning bet, one that applies most or all of the principles in this book.

So why does Company One hedge its bets? Because it doesn't understand tradeshow marketing from A to Z. Company Two, on the other hand, has been doing it for years, keeping its employees' knowledge base filled, continuing to experiment and innovate, and fully understanding what it takes.

Throughout this book, you'll learn how to dominate your industry and niche like Company Two.

Step One Challenge

Answer the following questions, either by yourself or with your tradeshow team.

1. What are your main show goals and objectives?
2. What is your secondary objective?
3. Who in your company defines your goals and objectives?
4. How well do you meet those goals with your tradeshow marketing?
5. Understanding that each tradeshow has a different target market and a different mix of attendees, how do your goals and objectives change from show to show?
6. What is your target audience?
7. Does this show meet that target?
8. Which companies are your main competitors at the show?

9. How do they stack up against you in terms of the following:
    a. Booth size and scope
    b. Presence (show sponsorship, other advertising opportunities)
    c. Staffing
    d. Preshow marketing
    e. Market and branding visibility

DOLLARS, POUNDS, EUROS: HOW MUCH DO YOU REALLY NEED TO MAKE THIS WORK?

Money—it makes the tradeshow world go around. So let's visit some numbers from the tradeshow floor.

- Visitors spend an average of 8.3 hours across 2.3 days on a tradeshow floor, giving exhibitors the chance to reach thousands of potential customers in a very short time (Center for Exhibition Industry Research [CEIR], 2008).

- 39 percent of visitors come to the same show at least two years in a row, providing exhibitors with a loyal base of committed potential customers (CEIR, 2008).
- 50 percent of attendees already have a buying plan when attending shows (CEIR, 2007).
- Decision makers love exhibitions: 87 percent of survey respondents state that national exhibitions represent an "extremely useful" source of needed purchasing information (CEIR, 2004).

On average, tradeshows account for one-third of a company's annual marketing budget. Much of that money is simply flushed down the drain. Why? Because many company tradeshow and exhibit managers don't have a thorough, detailed plan for each show and often the booth staff is unaware of the reasons for even being at the show, other than the generic "business-building" excuse.

The event industry is on the rise, though, and companies continue to pay out for tradeshows, committing significant portions of marketing budgets to lead-gathering and branding activities. Since the 2008 recession, most industries and events have seen climbing attendance figures.

Tradeshow marketing is probably the one marketing activity that demands precise accounting procedures; without that attention to detail, it's easy for money to slip away, no one knowing where it went or why it's gone. It's also the least forgiving activity in terms of return on investment if the principal players don't watch *how* that money is spent.

Having said that, good tradeshow marketing doesn't mean you have to spend hundreds of thousands of dollars. It does mean, though, that the dollars you do spend should be carefully funneled to the most appropriate spots.

This step is about numbers. I figured we'd better get it out of the way, so you can move on to the fun stuff in steps three and beyond.

So what about the numbers?

Booth Budget

For whatever reason, your company has come to the conclusion that it's time for a new tradeshow display. It could be that your old booth is just worn out. Perhaps you need a complete makeover to show the world what the company is really like these days. Or maybe you've outgrown the old booth. Whatever the reason, you need something new.

How do you determine how much to spend? And beyond that, how much *should* you spend for what you really want or need?

When sitting down with a tradeshow exhibit consultant, you'll cover many issues such as, does the budget include show services, storage, crating, setup, and dismantle, or just the design and fabrication of the display?

In consultation with exhibitors, one question is always lurking, and whether it's stated clearly or not, it's almost always there: "Why do exhibits cost so much?"

The question comes up with companies that are looking to make a big splash at their next appearance, and they are considering a fabricated, custom-designed booth. They've seen some creative exhibits at recent shows and are coveting such an impactful presentation for their company. So they look into getting such a booth with Company A and come away with what can charitably be called sticker shock.

So they look at another company, thinking that Company A's pricing must be outrageous, only to find that Companies B, C, and D have similar pricing structure.

So what are the factors that go into the cost of a custom-designed and fabricated booth, particularly one conveying the impression that its owners barred no expense? After all, when interested companies learn they could routinely spend a quarter of a million dollars on a custom 40' x 50' booth, they think, "I could build a heckuva house for that money that would last a couple of hundred years!" Booths hardly last that long, however. They may last five to seven years, though, and, depending on the company's needs and budgets, they often earn their money back several times over.

But just like that custom house that requires a general contractor, architect, plumber, roofer, electrician, and so forth, a custom exhibit generally requires a three-dimensional (3-D) booth designer, a graphic designer, a production/fabrication team, and a skilled project manager to guide everything from start to finish.

Costs easily add up, with the biggest cost typically being skilled labor. Everyone, in fact, is a skilled and trained craftsman who expects to be paid well for their work. It's a good bet that when you hire a team, you are paying for access to expertise that adds up to dozens, if not hundreds, of years of combined skill in design, fabrication, project management, and production.

You're often paying as well for warranties ensuring that, as years go by, things that break under the continuing challenges of packing, setting up, and shipping will be fixed with a smile and nominal (or no) fee. You could buy a lower-cost version of the same exhibit on the Internet and save 20, 30, or 40 percent. But what happens when something breaks down on the imported booth and you need to replace a part?

All of those items—design, fabrication, graphic design and production, crating, storage, shipping—mean that, yes, your exhibit can end up costing *a lot*. But if you're prepared, you can budget for that creative, attractive, and functional exhibit and get it when you can afford it.

Justifying the Cost of a New Booth

When it's time for a new booth, how do you justify the cost?

There are many ways to look at the expense, and getting management to come on board to approve the investment is often one of the biggest challenges you may have. *You* may be firmly convinced that the investment is justified, but how do you convince management that it's a good investment?

Let's walk through a few things that I believe will assist in your quest to convince management that it's a worthwhile cost.

First, can you point to tradeshow marketing as a consistent method of bringing in leads and generating brand awareness? Are you turning those leads into clients? If that's true, you can validate the premise that tradeshow marketing is a critical piece of the company's marketing expenses.

However, if that's the case, the next question may be, why do you need to fix it? Isn't it already working?

It may indeed be working. But if you're consistently running into issues such as growth, lack of space, and too many visitors in such a small space, it may be that you are in need of a bigger space and hence, a bigger booth. One way to determine this is to track visitors by counting, or by anecdotal evidence from your booth staff.

If tradeshow marketing is a solid and consistent business driver, it's likely that the people with the purse strings may be sympathetic to the request.

Second, consider the prospect of *not* doing anything. What would happen if you did *not* invest in a new booth? Are you satisfied with holding firm with the current booth property? The questions that come up around this question include how old the current asset is, and how is it being perceived by your staff and clients at the show.

Another part of this conundrum is this: what are your most direct competitors doing? If the top three competitors in your market have upgraded and upsized their booth properties in the last two or three years, the perception will be that you're losing ground to them. And in a competitive market, perception is critical.

Third, do your research. What are your competitors doing? What are the strengths, weaknesses, opportunities, and threats from within and without? A simple SWOT Analysis, as discussed briefly in step one, can tell you a lot about where you are and where you might go from here.

Fourth, ask yourself if a new booth is really the answer. What about investing in your booth staff instead or in preshow marketing and postshow follow-up? Support your staff with training and education that allows them to more properly interact on the show floor with attendees by asking the right questions. Maybe a booth isn't really right yet, but a smaller investment in the staff may yield good results without the larger booth investment, which can then be put off a year or two or three.

Fifth, if a new booth is the answer, spend some time assessing how to understand the investment of capital, what's involved, when it will be delivered, and how it will happen. This will likely mean talking with booth designers and fabricators to get an idea of how much time and money it would cost to develop a design and construct the booth.

Sixth, once these items are assembled, they should be presented in the context of the life of the booth. Do you plan to use the booth for three, five, or seven years before considering major upgrades? In the case of one client who had committed to a 30' x 30' island booth in 2012, they had an opportunity to upgrade the space at a major expo in 2015 to a 30' x 40', and decided the investment of a 10' x 30' addition was worth it.

Seventh, determine how the new booth will change those who are tasked with the logistics of setting up and dismantling the booth, staffing it for the shows, and inviting more clients for one-on-one meetings. In my experience, upgrading to a larger booth will modestly impact the marketing staff, giving them more opportunities to meet more clients and spread the word about the booth. Costs for setup and dismantle will rise. Shipping costs will rise. Stepping up to a new booth is a major commitment, but it can often be well worth it in the return on that investment.

Eighth, now it's time to present the final proposed cost. Assemble your pitch using the elements above. Make it more engaging with visuals by creating graphs showing the increased reach or potential booth designs by grabbing booth renderings from online examples. Schedule time with management and make sure they understand what you're proposing. Use whatever combination of these methods you think will work best for you.

You've assembled a design and fabrication team that is capable. You have a reasonable price range for the project and know the time frame necessary to accomplish the task. While the bean counters will want to justify the case in hard dollars won versus dollars spent, in addition to showing how the cost will be justified by the return with new business, detail the "soft" return. These soft reasons to spend the money may include increased business opportunities due to a larger booth, more visibility at the shows, easier and quicker setup times, perception of being bigger and better than your competitors, better branding opportunities in your booth, and so on. Be as specific as possible. For instance, "Our new booth will give us a 300 percent increase in visible graphic display area to show off our brand and products compared with our current display."

Once the presentation is over, if management doesn't immediately open their checkbooks (!), ask for a hard decision within a certain time frame. No doubt they'll have questions and want to discuss the issue. Who knows, maybe they love the idea and were just looking for justification themselves! Or perhaps they need to push the action to later in the year. In any case, you've made your pitch, and if you did your homework, it was a good, professional pitch!

If you're entering the "we're getting a new custom booth" phase, when you first sit down with a 3-D booth designer, you'll have to lay everything on the table and be candid about how much you're able to spend.

It's a bit like planning to purchase a new car and not knowing how much you have to spend. If you did, you probably wouldn't ask for all the options without considering the costs. The car you describe may cost $65,000, but with only $30,000 to spend, you'd feel chagrined and embarrassed. The opposite is also true: If you wanted a budget car that cost only $19,000, but put $45,000 on the table, the salesperson would be a little shocked and do his or her best to upgrade you to a luxury car that you may not want or need.

It's the same with a tradeshow booth. Your discussion with your exhibit consultant should be candid, with transparent plans to cover all costs so that when your management team approves the money, they know exactly what they're buying. Not only that, but once the budget is clear, the designer has the responsibility to design something that fits the budget.

Having a realistic budget number is important for both buyer and seller. Where does that realistic number come from?

Start with the floor space. If you're upgrading from a 10' x 10' to a 10' x 20', you'll first need to know the cost of the floor space.

Next, determine the cost of show services (setup, dismantle, cleaning, padding and carpet rental, hanging signs, and so forth).

Now determine the cost of manpower: staffing, lead generation, and management.

When all of these numbers are compiled, you have arrived at the all-inclusive cost of your booth.

It could be that you've determined all of the above. Still, you should know that there are additional costs.

Booth budgets can spring from either renting or buying a booth. In extremely general terms, a custom exhibit booth purchase goes for around $1,000 per linear foot for inline booths and about $135–$150 per square foot for island booths, a price that includes design and fabrication. Those industry averages have crept upward in the past decade, but not substantially, and they are still good numbers for ballpark budgeting purposes.

That means your new 10' x 10' booth will likely cost about $10,000 and your 10' x 20' booth will come in at about $20,000. Of course, these are starting numbers; your mileage may vary.

While you can get a booth at virtually any exhibit house, there are many display and customizing alternatives to choose from. Depending on the show, it might make sense to build something in-house, from repurposed and recycled materials. Many companies in the natural food and outdoor industries like to show off their earth-friendly bona fides, which might mean making tables out of car hoods, exhibit walls from wooden pallets, or using shipping crates as tables. Getting a custom-built booth is great, but don't limit yourself. Creativity should be applied to healthy budgets as well as the thinnest ones.

Now that you know some basics, the next step is to sit down with an exhibit booth consultant and discuss all of the parameters of the booth: function, storage, display space, graphic messaging, monitors, meeting space, and so forth. A good consultant will go over each of these in detail.

Step Two Challenge

Sit down with your marketing team to answer the following questions. If you already don't know all the answers, you and your team will learn a lot as you tackle these questions.

1. What is your annual tradeshow marketing budget?
2. What percentage of the company's overall marketing budget does the tradeshow marketing segment comprise?
3. Who determines what the annual tradeshow marketing budget is?
4. How often does that assessment take place?
5. Is that budget amount known throughout the company?
6. Is the budget increasing, decreasing, or staying about the same?
7. Is your current budget sufficient?

Complete a breakdown of the annual budget by show, and then break down each show by space rental, shipping/handling/drayage expenses, booth repair and upgrades, travel/lodging, promotions, giveaways, product samples, and other miscellaneous costs.

What is the company's decision-making process for creating a new tradeshow booth?

Does your company's marketplace success directly impact your tradeshow marketing budget and vice versa?

Here is a list of items to include in your budget. Be sure to download our free Excel spreadsheet (find the link in the appendix).

- Booth design and construction
- Show services
- Booth personnel
- Advertising and marketing
- Shipping
- Lead gathering
- Postshow sales data: leads, cost per lead, number of known sales, average amount of each sale, return on investment, miscellaneous

Once you have these numbers, archive them (more in step eleven). You'll be glad you have these numbers as the shows and years go on.

GETTING READY FOR THE BIG DANCE

Time to meet fictional exhibitor number two, Wally, who's the head of business development for a company called Pharaoh, which manufactures energy bars and natural snacks. In the thirty years since the company launched, Wally has helped it grow from a small player to the dominant company in the market that it is today. He maintains they couldn't have done it without tradeshow marketing.

Wally is fiftyish, married, has two grown kids, and drives a new Audi that is provided by the company. He's worked for Pharaoh for twenty-five years, joining it shortly after it began to see double-digit growth in its fifth year.

After five decades on the planet and going on three decades with the same company, not much fazes Wally, certainly not the fact that his glasses keep getting thicker or that his hair is getting thinner. His pleasant, upbeat manner makes him a friend to all.

When it comes to preshow marketing, Wally knows what works for him and what doesn't. He is a master of delegation. He works with a small marketing team, but he brings in an outside agency for critical media outreach (see step twelve). None of which means he isn't interested in trying new things—he just has to be convinced that something is a worthwhile investment, and he doesn't stray too far from the mainstream. After all, that's where Pharaoh's market lies. When it comes to tradeshow marketing, Wally is conservative, but not so conservative that he isn't interested in the new things that might be worth trying.

The following conversation is imaginary.

"So, Wally, tell me about Pharaoh's preshow marketing."

"Sure thing," said Wally. "We do two large expos a year, so we place more importance on those than the smaller shows.

"We set up the founder of the company, Phil, with media interviews for each show. Even though he's in his seventies, he loves the attention and, truthfully, he knows both the company and the new products better than anyone. Plus, he's the face of the company, so people expect his presence."

"What are you trying to do with those media interviews?"

"Generally speaking, secure as many write-ups as possible. But we also like to filter in health-related items, such as new research on the food products that we produce being beneficial to the heart and similar things. There's always new stuff out there that applies to our products, so we have to keep a watch out for that," Wally said.

"What else?"

"Phil wrote a book a couple of years ago, and we always have book signings and photo ops with him. Not only that, he's an avid outdoorsman, so we like to bring some part of his outdoor life into the show. Maybe a short video of a recent ski trip or some mountain he climbed. But we want to strike a fine balance. He's the everyday working guy, so we can't show that he's gallivanting around the world all the time. Instead, he needs to appear as hardworking as the people who buy the products. It's all about showing the benefits of a healthy lifestyle, so there are a lot more people in the videos than just Phil."

"What about other preshow planning? What do you want folks' main takeaway from the show to be?" I asked.

"We really aren't at the big expo shows to sell products. We want our distributors to see us, to give our brokers a chance to take part, to do media, and to generally show our competitors that if they want to catch us, they have a long ways to go."

There goes a confident man with a plan!

However, as confident as Wally sounds, he knows that it takes effort to stay on top. Much of the company's effort is focused on carving out a slightly larger space each year, which explains why the company gradually progressed from a 10' x 10' to a 10' x 30' to a 20' x 20', then a 20' x 30', then a 30' x 30', and currently a 40' x 40' space at the larger expos.

"You can't stay on top by sitting still," Wally says.

"So what goes into preshow preparations?"

"There's preshow marketing and promotion [which is covered in another step], staff training [covered in another step], booth preparation, product and service preparation, show research, generating public relations [another step], engaging social media [another step], sales and lead-generation prep, and so much more."

"So where do you start?"

"As my old writing professor used to say, 'Start anywhere. Begin now.'"

And that's important, especially for those of us not as well organized as others.

And while organization is important, it's not the only thing.

For now, though, let's leave social media, the booth, and sales and lead generation for future steps. We'll instead focus on the twin tasks of publicizing your show appearance and drawing traffic to your booth.

Target Market

Remember in step one, where you defined your goals for the tradeshow? Of course you do. If you don't know your show goals, you'll be wasting time and money.

If, for instance, your company manufactures cutting-edge guitars and you're exhibiting at the Consumer Electronics Show (CES), your main goal might be to garner another dozen distributors and three endorsements from well-known guitar players.

To attain those results, it would take a stellar tradeshow booth, and it would take being at the *right* show. But it would also take an understanding of who your potential distributors are and whether they're attending.

If over half of your business is in the home-consumer sector, you likely have a good understanding of the industry, who the players are, and which distributors attend the CES.

In this case, it would mean targeting a number of those distributors, say fifty to seventy-five, if you want to obtain a dozen secure leads, and approaching them in a certain way that gets them to commit to come to your booth.

While a phone call or e-mail may be an easy way to contact them, neither is memorable. On the other hand, putting together a limited, snail-mail "plonk" campaign may make you stick out.

What's a plonk campaign? It's a piece of mail that makes a big *plonk* when it hits the recipient's desk. People love the plonk because it's hefty, tangible, and mysterious: What's in the damn package? So they rip it open and find that you've sent a soccer ball signed by Team USA, which whets their appetites and entices them to come to your booth.

A good creative agency can help you craft an inspired mailer that will connect the dots between the plonk piece and getting its recipients to your tradeshow booth. And if you're targeting only fifty potential clients, you can probably afford to be a bit extravagant and creative in crafting plonk mail that makes your company memorable. If, on the other hand, you're trying to reach a thousand potential clients or distributors, an extravagant plonk piece may be inappropriate and more expensive than you can afford.

In that case, you're left to other, lower-cost marketing approaches: e-mail blasts, online website ads that either promote or mention the show, postcards, or other direct mail pieces. A good social media campaign can also yield results.

If you desire to catch a bigger fish as well as a few thousand guppies, you can try a mix of direct mail, social media, e-mail blasts, and personal outreach, if convenient, such as phone calls and visits.

E-Mail

Your company no doubt has an e-mail list of clients, customers, and potential customers that you regularly contact. This is likely your most valuable marketing asset.

With a valuable list, whether it's 200, 20,000, or 200,000, you can craft a series of messages before the show that lets recipients know about new products you'll have on hand for demonstration, special guests or special deals, and contests or giveaways.

Most sophisticated e-mail marketing programs or companies have the ability to segment their e-mail lists and target specific messages to specific groups. If you're looking for a good automated e-mailing program, investigate Mail Chimp, Constant Contact, or AWeber. They all provide flexibility and increasing sophistication.

Your contact list might be broken down into the following:

- Established clients
- New clients
- Recent prospects
- Older prospects
- Potential clients

Each targeted message would be written specifically for one of these specific segments. For instance, you could invite current customers to come to the booth for a free software upgrade to your latest and greatest version. New clients might get an invitation to a small presentation off-site showing upcoming products to be released in six months. Potential clients would get an invitation for a special gift, such as a wine case, a leather writing pad, or a similarly impressive item that will keep your company "top of mind" when they get back to the office.

It's the same with direct marketing. If you only have mailing addresses for the bulk of your contact list, it might make sense to create a clever direct mail piece inviting them to your booth at the show.

Work with a professional promotional products consultant, and together you can create a unique premium gift offer, like that signed soccer ball inscribed with "Come see us at booth 2034!" that is nearly impossible to refuse.

Phone

The phone is so old fashioned, isn't it? However, it's personal in a way that social media and e-mail aren't. The only thing more personal, in fact, is an in-person visit. And if you can't make an in-person visit, a phone call is the next-best thing, except for perhaps a video call via Google Hangouts, Adobe Connect, GoToMeeting, or some other such platform.

Once you have identified several people who you'd like to stop by the booth at your upcoming show, call them. Let them know specifically what they'll find at the show. If appropriate, schedule a meeting with one of your key salespeople or management reps. By making it personal, and by scheduling a meeting (and confirming it shortly before the show), you've significantly increased the chances by a huge factor that they'll come to your booth.

It's said that even in this digital age, face-to-face events are growing and thriving. People love meeting one another in person. Take advantage of that. Schedule appointments. Meet people. Ask questions and answer questions. Get to know folks better. Shake hands, pat them on the back, make a deal, part with a smile.

Social Media

We'll cover social media engagement more extensively in step eight, but let's spend a few brief moments considering it here.

Social media is perfect for tradeshows, events, and conferences. Twitter, especially, is great for drawing attention to events and happenings in real time. Other than picking up a telephone and calling *everyone*, there is no better way to alert people to something that's happening *right now*.

A few years ago, I walked a back aisle at a large tradeshow when several people ran past me, laughing and yelling. I caught the word "twitter," so I pulled up Twitter, found the show hashtag, and saw that a booth in the back of the hall had sent out a tweet saying that they had some free hats for the first dozen people to the booth. It caused a mini-stampede!

Social media works. Does it always work for every situation? No, nothing is that bulletproof—not e-mail, direct mail, phone calls, or in-person visits. But a timely tweet can catch the attention of tradeshow visitors and move them to action.

Facebook is better for showing both what you have coming up and what just happened, but it's not so good for getting someone's immediate attention. Facebook's mysterious algorithms mean that most people won't see your post in real time. Instead, they'll see posts based on their recent history of clicks, likes, and interactions.

Facebook, though, can be valuable, through the generous use of photos and videos, in displaying the activities in your booth. Twitter, on the other hand, is an immediate sensation. You can see tweets in real time and can search hashtags by the most recent postings.

Although you can certainly post photos and videos on either platform, Facebook tends to have more of a friendly, town-square feeling, whereas Twitter gives the impression of a thousand people shouting to be heard.

Twitter's 140-character-per-tweet limit has both positive and negative aspects. It forces you to craft a quick, digestible tweet, but the downside is that it invites people to share short thoughts that may deserve more, well, thought.

If your product or service is photo friendly, it makes sense to consider further social media options, such as Pinterest, Instagram, and Vine. All are image driven and popular. If you are unfamiliar with these social media platforms, spend a few moments investigating others' use of them for some good ideas.

Once plugged into a social media platform, it's not difficult to get the hang of it, nor does it have to consume a lot of time. Posting a photo on Twitter takes only a few moments; posting on Instagram and Pinterest takes a few more.

Again, look to step eight for more ideas on social media engagement as you prepare for events, tradeshows, and conferences.

Bottom line: If you want to have a successful tradeshow appearance, leave as little to chance as possible. Schedule and confirm appointments. Plan and execute your preshow marketing. Make notes, debrief, and tweak your processes for the next time.

Step Three Challenge

Pull your team together again. Discuss the following questions and make notes where pertinent.

1. Who is your target market?
2. How will you reach them before the show?

E-mail

1. How far in advance of the show do you e-mail your market?
2. How many times do you e-mail them before the show?
3. What's your message—is it product or service related?

Social Media

1. What platforms do you use to promote the show?
    Twitter, Facebook, LinkedIn, YouTube, Pinterest, or others?
    Direct Mail?
    Telephone?
    Other?
2. What's your message to the market?
3. What top products or services are you promoting at the next show?
4. When do you typically roll out your preshow marketing?
5. How often do you communicate with your market prior to the show?
    1–2 times
    3–5 times
    ≥6 times

DID YOU COME TO THE RIGHT DANCE?

You've spent thousands of dollars to either rent or purchase a booth. In addition, you've paid a pretty penny for the booth space, you've ponied up for plane tickets for staffers, and you've lodged them a few blocks from the show.

But what if you're at the *wrong show*?

Before we review whether you're *truly* attending the right show(s), let's clarify some issues surrounding show exhibiting.

Many exhibitors keep going to the same show year after year. Why? Because they've always gone. When I attend shows, I often ask exhibitors, "Why are you at this specific show? What do you want to get out of it?"

Many exhibitors have an answer at their fingertips. Some don't, and they appear puzzled by the question. If they appear puzzled by the question, there's a good chance they'll be even more puzzled by their own answers.

So let's examine the concept of attending the right shows, attending *only* the right shows, and *not* going to shows that don't make sense.

Our fictional marketing director, Katie, of Gotcha! Cookies 'n' Treats, offers these thoughts:

"We had a pretty good idea of which shows to attend, but we wanted to make sure they were good investments. So the owner, Beth, and I attended four shows in one year. We asked questions, talked to exhibitors, found out what they thought of those shows, gathered cost information, and eventually decided to exhibit at three of the shows the next year.

"Before we committed to any of them, we had a pretty good idea of the audience, and how our small company would fit in with other exhibitors.

We don't mind being next to competition—it shows we're all at the right show. If we had no competitors selling cookies or other baked treats, we probably shouldn't be at that particular show."

Katie took the words out of my mouth. If I had been asked to advise an exhibitor on how to determine which shows to go to, that is exactly what I would say.

Spend some time online searching for similar shows. Check the appendix for exhibit industry search tools.

Map of Shows

To get started, make a list of all the shows that you currently exhibit at each year. These would include large national tradeshows, smaller regional shows, and any local or city shows. With this list, you're ready to move the bar higher.

Next, list any shows that you used to attend, but haven't for a few years. Note how long it's been since you've exhibited at any given one.

Now make a list of industry shows that you might consider attending.

Finally, research and list any shows peripheral to your industry. For instance, if you sell healthy grains, there may be shows in the health or medical industries that nurses, doctors, and educators attend, where you can set up a small educational booth.

At this point, depending on your industry, you'll either have a list of a lot of shows or one of just a few. It doesn't matter. We're just getting a lay of the land, so to speak.

Now it's time to determine if your target audience attends these shows. There are several ways to do this. Often, show organizers offer a breakdown of attendees at their shows. Some sets of information are more detailed than others, but most show websites offer at least a rudimentary breakdown of attendees and exhibitors.

For instance, the Southeast Natural Products Association's show site looks like this:

- 38 percent Grocery
- 39 percent Supplements
- 15 percent Powdered food
- 8 percent Other (personal, pet, household, appliances, and so forth)

While there's little about the actual attendees here, the breakdown of exhibitors into categories gives you some clues about the type of attendance.

One more example: At the Natural Products Northwest Show in Seattle, there's a lengthy description of the show on the tradeshow search site, TSNN.com.

We learn that the show entails "dietary supplements, homeopathy, sustainable/green living, retail business solutions, natural and organic products, aromatherapy, healthy lifestyle accessories, appliances-equipment, food and beverage, sports nutrition, health-related products, health and beauty aids, pet products, books and publications, gift items."

That's a pretty good description of who's going to be there. So what about the attendees? Any help here?

"The NW show is open to ALL retailers of natural products and open to all store formats. We welcome not only independent food stores, but also chains and crossover stores. To boost attendance, we encourage non-members to attend including buyers from airlines, schools and industry-affiliated organizations."

Well, that helps. One more tidbit jumps out from the show description: "Festive tradeshow with 175+ exhibitors...." That tells me that it's a relatively small show, especially when you consider that national shows in

Anaheim, Las Vegas, and New York City draw a few thousand exhibitors. Still, it might be something to put on your "needs more research" list.

One short, effective way to determine if a show is appropriate for you is to look at the list of exhibitors. If your main competitors are there (and you're not), there's a pretty good chance that you should be there, too.

But who's to know if that show is working for them? If the biggest exhibitors keep expanding their booths over the years, it's a good bet they're seeing positive results.

And if you want to find out if a particular show is working for those competitors, what's wrong with picking up the phone and calling a few of them?

"I see you're still exhibiting at the _____ show. I'm curious if you think that show is a good investment for you."

That's blatantly straightforward and will often work. However, if that's not your style, you can try sneaking up with a more indirect approach: "Hey, I'm looking into finding out about the _____ show. I understand you've exhibited there for a few years. What's been your experience there?"

If you call an exhibitor who is not a direct competitor (you sell cookies; they sell dog treats), chances are you will get some good intel about the show.

Making the Leap

Tradeshow exhibiting at the right show can be extraordinarily beneficial for a company's bottom line. By talking to other exhibitors, digging into the show's attendee and exhibit profiles, and researching the show website, you can judge the show's usefulness to you.

But even if the show *seems* like a no-brainer, it may not actually be. For example, it may be such a high-cost, high-profile national show that your small company will look and feel out of place. On the other hand, if the investment is handled right, making your debut at that high-cost, high-profile national show might be just what your company needs to jump-start business into new markets.

And it's not always just about the show. Other factors will determine whether it's the right show for you. If your production capacity is stretched thin, for example, you'll have to decide if and how you can ramp up your production to meet new demands.

Making the leap from a small company to serving a national or international market involves much more than simply picking the right tradeshows. It means a critical self-examination, checking to see if you and your employees are ready for it. If done right, though, putting your goods and services on display at a national tradeshow can effectively expose you to bigger markets and wider audiences.

Going national or international also exposes your company to different audiences and cultures. What will be their response be to your products or services? Yes, it's an international, one-world planet we live on. Cultures mesh, languages adapt, people move across lines easily. But what is big in Taiwan may not be worth much in Billings, Montana. Reaching new markets is the easy part, relatively speaking. Making sure your company is prepared for those new markets—in aspects such as production, attitude, and education—is much harder.

Step Four Challenge

Go through the various questions presented here with your team. Get answers from show resources when you can. For the more subjective questions, ask each team member to write down answers so everyone may discuss and reach a consensus.

1. What's the potential audience at each show?
2. What's the potential audience for the whole year at all shows?
3. What's your potential lead harvesting at each show? For the whole year? (More on lead generation in step ten.)
4. What do you want to get out of the next show? What about the show after that?
5. How many leads would satisfy your goal?
6. How many media mentions are you angling for?

7. How much social media content can you get?
8. Which shows are best for creating content (videos, photos, contests, blog posts, and so forth)?
9. Which shows are the worst?
10. Which shows have the biggest potential to land a large client or customer?
11. Which shows are the most obviously beneficial to grow your business?

By discussing your answers internally, you'll gain insight into different ways to approach different shows, as well as help in coming up with more ideas for promotions, show research and surveys, and contests.

A few more items to consider: These questions will help you look at your tradeshow marketing from a different view. The first question may be one of those "duh" questions because you *know* what you're doing right. Right? But do you really? Writing it down helps you to internalize it.

1. In your opinion, what are the most obvious things you're doing right?
2. In your opinion, what are the most obvious things you're doing wrong?
3. If money were no object, what would your next tradeshow booth look like?
4. If you could take as many people you wanted to the show, how many would you take?
5. Which people would you take who don't currently go?
6. Which people currently go, but would you prefer to leave at home? (OK, this question may be for your eyes only.)
7. What's your *biggest company goal*? And how will tradeshow marketing impact that goal?

All of this information will help you discern whether you're going to the right shows. If you are participating in the right shows, then you're on the right track.

HOME IS WHERE THE BOOTH IS

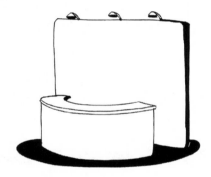

In step two, we explored the process of coming up with a realistic budget for a new tradeshow booth. Let's now turn to the various elements that make your new booth attractive, creative, and (most important) functional.

Brand

Let's start with the *brand*. Your booth should convey, at a glance, the look and feel of your brand. When a visitor sees your booth at the show, it should evoke a visceral reaction at first glance, based on the branding, materials, colors, and products on display. So how is that accomplished?

Let's explore booth branding on a midsize scale with Wally, our head of business development at Pharaoh. After six years presiding over a 20' x

20' booth that was bursting at the seams, the company decided to commit to a new, larger booth. According to Wally, the boss didn't like the way the space grew, but the old booth didn't look right in the larger space.

"We found that even though we had a larger space, the overall look and feel of the booth was becoming disjointed," said Wally.

"What options did you look at for the larger space?"

"The first option was to go back to our original designer and explore the idea of making adjustments to the old booth by adding new pieces. It quickly became clear that we'd spend a good chunk of money, but still have most of the old booth and a few new pieces.

"So the second option was to design a new booth from the ground up. It was clear early on that this was a much more attractive prospect, even though the cost was more," said Wally. "So we got to work with our long-time exhibit company. They had a new designer who, even though he was new to us, was very familiar with our brand."

"I'd agree," I said. "Generally, it takes a good designer who understands your company. Even if a designer doesn't know anything about your company, he or she'll want to spend time steeping him or herself in the company's advertising, products, branding, and interaction on various social media outlets."

"When we sat down with the new designer, to his credit, he asked a lot of good questions," explained Wally. "He asked if we could provide a one-page description that discussed look, feel, function, potential building materials, colors, meeting space requirements, storage, and even what products we thought we'd be promoting. Pretty easy for us to do, but I like the depth of detail he requested."

"Kind of like putting together an RFP [request for proposal] even though you'd already chosen a designer and exhibit fabricator, correct?" I asked.

"Exactly. When we did our first island booth several years ago, that's exactly what we did. We assembled an RFP and asked five companies to respond. From there, our current company offered the best response."

How do you accomplish the creation of a tradeshow booth that represents your brand to a tee?

For some, that's a natural wood look. For others, it means a high-tech look straight out of *Star Trek*. That doesn't mean that a rootsy, earth mama brand couldn't host an aluminum structure with fabric graphics. Those decisions are typically made through detailed conversations with a three-dimensional (3-D) booth designer, the company's marketing team, and an exhibit fabricator. Still, the goal should be that when a visitor sees the booth and the company's name, it evokes a *feeling* that is in congruence with what the company wants the visitor to feel. If it does not, somebody messed up.

An exhibit designer may be an accomplished 3-D designer, but not necessarily someone who is good at graphic design. Good graphic designers, meanwhile, don't necessarily have the skills to design a 3-D booth, which must take into consideration height, depth, traffic flow, shipping, setup and dismantle considerations, and more. And a good 3-D exhibit designer doesn't necessarily have the skills to design your booth graphics. These are two specialized skills, and you'll be better off working with separate designers for each.

Let's showcase an actual exhibitor, Rooibee Red Tea, to show how the process might work. Creative director Zachary Anderson was kind enough to discuss the company's approach to tradeshow marketing and share details of its approach.

For Rooibee Red Tea, showcasing the extensive heritage of the product was critical. At Expo West, they tea-bag dyed their foam floor, which was white. The tea dye was in the shape of the continent of Africa, which is where their tea is grown.

As Anderson explained, even though the tea is grown in Africa, it's brewed and packaged in Kentucky. The image on the floor is meant to show that "this is something exotic. We want to have some of those rustic roots come through."

In their 10' x 10' booth, the impact comes not so much from the booth, but from what they do in the booth. "We ask ourselves," Anderson relates, "'How can I make a bigger impact with the booth that I have?' Is everything being utilized to its full potential? What are you doing that is going to display your story to its fullest?"

For an independent brand, a tradeshow is a significant and important investment and, as Anderson says, "Knowing how to make the biggest impact in the space is very important."

Graphics

Most people don't think of their tradeshow graphics as being tasked with specific functions, but that's what is going on.

Imagine you're a tradeshow visitor. You have a couple of hours to walk the floor, and you're on the lookout for products to stock in your store or offer to your customers. You're walking at a decent pace, which means that each booth gets anywhere from three to seven seconds of your attention *at best.*

Three to seven seconds—at best. It's probably more like one to three seconds.

From an exhibitor's standpoint, this can be a big pain. If you don't clearly and quickly convey your company and product's messaging, you lose any chance to capture the attention of attendees.

The solution? Your graphics messaging must clearly communicate several items at a glance. The graphics are the most visually important part of your booth. Yes, you might have an attractive booth, but if the messaging is unclear, that attractiveness doesn't count for much.

Now that you know how important it is for your messaging to be clear, let's look at exactly what that means.

The messaging should do the following:

1. Attract attention.
2. Create intrigue or curiosity.
3. Qualify and/or disqualify visitors quickly.

Your graphic messaging should be planned. That means creating a graphics hierarchy that forces a natural progression of eye contact from higher to lower and left to right.

People will normally see something large, colorful, and high first, and then move on to the next lower and smaller item. A good designer will design your graphics accordingly.

If the graphics are doing their job, attendees will quickly and clearly see the intended message, which will either attract them because it's a potential match or repel them if it's not a match.

This means the hierarchy works like this:

1. Company Name or Logo (large and at the top)
2. Positioning Statement or Bold Challenge (smaller and second from the top)
3. Supporting Statement (smallest and at or below eye level)

However, if your company is not well known, this typical hierarchy might change a bit:

1. Bold Statement or Challenging Question
2. Company Name or Logo
3. Supporting Statement

On rare occasions, the company name might drop all the way to third place, that is, if it's an unknown company or if the company name is really insignificant:

1. Bold Statement or Challenging Question
2. Supporting Statement
3. Company Name or Logo

If your product or brand is more important or more recognizable than the company name, the hierarchy might look like this:

1. Brand
2. Tag Line or Positioning Statement
3. Supporting Statement

No one-size-fits-all approach for graphics on tradeshow booths covers all companies or situations. Instead, your goals, products, and objectives should determine how the graphic hierarchy is displayed. The main thing to remember is that visitors pass booths quickly, and they all become a blur. Imagine your booth is a freeway billboard and you have just a few quick seconds to catch someone's attention.

Let's return to the idea of qualifying and/or disqualifying a visitor from stopping at the booth with a simple message.

If your message is too generic, you'll attract people who don't fully understand your business. For instance, if the key message says "We Solve Business Problems," a visitor will think it's too bland and won't enter; they may misunderstand the problem you are solving.

On the other hand, "We Solve Large Shipping Problems with Instant Consultation" is clear. Your visitors will know what you do, and they will know right away if they are potential customers. Remember, people hate to be sold to, but they love to buy. If your positioning statement grabs attendees with a pointed and pertinent statement or bold question, they will slow down and consider stopping at the booth.

If the attendee is a shipping manager with daily shipping challenges, he or she will feel compelled to enter the booth to learn more. If attendees have nothing to do with shipping at their company, they will keep on moving.

By creating a specific selling statement, you've steered traffic either to or away from you. Once an attendee is self-selected, he or she will be easier to start a conversation with, by asking something like "Do you handle shipping for your company?"

Booth Function

When transitioning from a 10' x 10' exhibit to a larger island, function must be carefully determined. Show goals and objectives, the number of booth staff, and how you want to interact with visitors will determine function.

For example, if you're conducting product demonstrations, you'll need a booth big enough to accommodate the presenter or demonstrator and a small audience. If you're sampling edibles, on the other hand, perhaps all you'll need is an easy-to-reach sampling table.

Every booth is different, every show is different, and every company's goals and objectives are different. Other questions to settle are as follows:

- Do you have enough storage?
- How many meeting areas do you need?
- Should the meeting areas be completely private or only semiprivate?
- What products and/or services are you promoting at this show?
- Do you need video monitors or an iPad kiosk to help visitors interact?

Those needs can be determined by the experience you've had at past shows as well as conversations with your exhibit staff.

And no matter which functions you detail and prepare for in your booth, chances are good that once you've lived in the booth for a few days, you'll notice things that need to be changed for the next time. For example, a company had a 20' x 30' booth built that included a meeting space for its clients. One end of the booth, about an 8' x 20' space, initially was a covered meeting area, inaccessible to the casual visitor. After exhibiting in the booth just twice, it became apparent that client meetings weren't happening as often as anticipated. However, booth staffers did find it to be a quick and easy place to rest for a few moments. Those few moments soon turned into many minutes. Eventually, the covered meeting area was removed, and the space became better utilized for product display and visitor interaction.

Booth function also includes storage, meeting areas, and traffic flow. When planning a booth, you'll want to take these issues into account. That's not to say that they're often—or ever—overlooked, but it's not out of the ordinary for their costs to be miscalculated.

Storage: At minimum, you'll have to provide storage for personal items such as coats, purses, briefcases, laptops, and more. You may also need storage space for product display and more depending on your company's goals. Do you have enough space? Make sure you have enough, but don't overdo it! Space is at a premium at tradeshows, and every cubic inch needs to be considered.

Traffic flow: Do visitors have easy access to the inside of the booth? Or alternatively, do you even want them to have easy access? Some companies design booths so that only desired visitors are allowed inside, limiting access to the casual attendees. Others want any and all visitors to step across the line.

Meeting areas: How many staffers will be meeting with clients or media at the booth? How often? How many meetings are already scheduled in advance? How many do you anticipate to happen randomly?

Truthfully, it's quite possible that the needs of any given show will shift slightly from previous shows. The best approach is to pay attention to how the booth is used and make adjustments as budgets and goals shift.

Logistics, Setup, and Dismantle

One new client insisted that its display *had* to ship in a case small enough to go by UPS or FedEx. Large 4' x 4' x 8' wooden crates were a big *no-no,* it insisted. Every display discussed from that point forward had to meet that objective.

To this client, setup meant having a couple of booth staffers arrive a day or two early, setting up the booth with minimum fuss and tools. This would avoid the double-whammy costs of show labor and preshow staging and advance arrival at the warehouse.

For other companies, it's more important to show audiences a great booth that can accommodate a larger product display or demonstration area along with several meeting areas. That may mean a booth 40' x 40' or bigger requiring a day to set up, even with hired help, and that takes multiple crates to ship.

Any good exhibit company works with you to determine the best and most cost-effective solution.

Step Five Challenge

Below are questions to answer, ponder, and discuss when considering a new booth or upgrades to current property:

1. What is the size of your booth for your biggest show(s) each year?
2. How old is the booth?
3. Approximately how many times a year do you exhibit with this booth?
4. Do you have another booth or exhibit for smaller shows?
5. What is the best thing about your booth? The worst thing?
6. Does it truly and fully represent your brand? In other words, when people see it, do they think immediately of your product or company?
7. Does it have all of the functional needs that you desire?
8. What have you added or subtracted since you first used the booth? In other words, what have you tried to improve?
9. When do you think you will seriously consider either upgrading to a new booth or doing a major overhaul of your current booth? What's holding you back from doing it now?
10. What are the main functions of your booth?
    a. Product sampling
    b. Product demos
    c. Client meetings
    d. Branding

     e. Other

11. What is your lead-generation system?
     l.   Electronic
     m. Paper
     n. Other

12. Do you have other electronic interactivity in your booth?
     m. iPad
     n. Games
     o. Other

13. How well do your graphics convey your message?
14. Who designs your tradeshow graphics?
15. Are you satisfied with your tradeshow graphics design?
16. If you're not satisfied, how can they be improved?

Product or Service Demonstrations/Presentations

1. How do you show off your product?
2. Do you do product demonstrations in your booth?
3. Does your product or service lend itself well to in-booth demonstrations?
4. If so, do you hire professional presenters?
   a. If so, how well did that work for you?
   b. If not, have you considered hiring outside professional presenters?

IS YOUR FRONTLINE TEAM UP TO SNUFF?

You have a good booth, and your preshow planning and marketing is first rate. Your products are great. The show booth traffic is steady.

Yet, your results are flat, and you don't know why.

This is when many tradeshow managers scratch their heads, because in their minds, they're doing all they can do and doing it right. But it's not working. Could it be that the booth staff isn't prepared? Is it possible that the wrong booth staffers are going to the show? Let's look closer at what it takes to prepare a top-notch booth staff.

Booth Personnel

Who are you taking to staff the booth?

Every staffer should be outgoing, intelligent, approachable, friendly, and knowledgeable—or if they're lacking in one of those qualities, they should be able to fake it for a couple of days. Some people are naturally introverted, but they are able to turn it on and do a great job when required. Others are naturally extroverted, and they are always ready.

Consider that a tradeshow is typically a multiday event and that by the close, even the best staffers are feeling achy and tired. Not only should your staffers be prepared and trained in the skills of interaction with show attendees, but they should also be trained in the company's goals for this particular show.

"Well, duh," you say. That's a given.

But it's not out of the ordinary for exhibitors to send employees simply out of convenience, meaning staffers are ill-prepared for the show.

It's possible, and probably likely, that in such cases booth staffers aren't up to the task or haven't been properly trained or prepared to appear in a tradeshow booth.

A tradeshow floor is a fast-moving, chaotic environment. There may be thousands of exhibitors and tens of thousands of attendees. Even in smaller shows, the basics are still important. For instance, are you taking only your best salespeople? That may seem like a logical choice. However, a typical salesperson with no tradeshow-floor experience or training may not realize how different the situation is. He or she may have experience with "typical" sales situations, meaning setting up appointments, making office visits, and scheduling thirty-, sixty-, or ninety-minute meetings with prospects, depending on the time necessary for presentation.

That approach will not fly on the tradeshow floor. In fact, the typical sales approach works against your goal of moving people quickly through the booth, qualifying and disqualifying, so that you're spending maximum time with the best prospects and politely moving the tire kickers efficiently through.

Booth staffers should be prepared to ask specific questions, both in a pleasant manner and so they don't sound canned, yet still quickly engage visitors to determine if they are likely customers.

The idea of moving people along quickly doesn't mean, however, that you have to rush people. With the proper questions, you can clearly identify those who are good prospects and those who aren't. Recognition of attendees you must spend time with, as well as those who aren't going to buy, is a crucial tradeshow skill.

Based on tradeshow booth graphics, a visitor's self-selection process kicks in before he or she ever approaches the booth (see step five's section on booth graphics). However, staffers must be able to quickly distinguish between the two types, and recognize that even visitors who are not qualified have the ability to refer potential clients, which is why politeness is paramount. Graciously interacting with visitors, even those who are not prospects, may be key in prompting them to send business your way at some future date.

Wally, our intrepid twenty-five-year man with Pharaoh, believes branded shirts are an important tool. In fact, his company's employees wear them in the office back home.

"We decided long ago that it's important for people to recognize our company everywhere. We provide branded long-sleeve shirts for all employees, and our employees wear them at all times on the job.

"In fact, we make sure we wear them on the plane. You never know when you'll have a chance to make an impression on someone," said Wally.

Training

Andy Saks, owner and leader trainer with Spark Presentation, has a stated goal of "Helping you make more money by making better presentations." He's also experienced in training booth staff on how to interact with visitors.

"Booth staffers from virtually any company and in any situation will likely benefit from training," said Andy.

"What exactly would be expected from a training session?" I asked.

"That depends. A professional trainer will focus on getting staffers to understand the particular show and how the company's goals relate to exhibiting at that show."

According to Andy, a study at the show includes show metrics and the expected demographics of the attendees.

"We'll also brainstorm a profile of your target attendee and go over their job title, find out what their biggest challenges are, and give you the skill to recognize them fast," said Andy.

"Beyond that, our training will walk staffers through the steps of attracting, qualifying, demonstrating the products or services, and making sure that the relationship is extended by setting the next meeting, phone call, or e-mail."

Finally, a good training session will force staffers to practice and engage in role-playing situations.

Ken Newman, owner of Magnet Productions, says, "It's important that booth staff know how to approach strangers without being obnoxious. It's one of the best skills that a staffer can have."

Saks and Newman have conducted multiple booth staff trainings over the years and have the data (and testimonials) to prove that booth staff training is a key, if not the most important, element to exhibiting success.

Let's touch base with someone who has worked with Andy, Ann Derby of INIT USA, an international company using tradeshows as one tool to promote its work with intelligent transportation systems.

Ann told me that before they hired Andy and Spark Presentation to train her staffers, her colleagues felt they really didn't need the training.

"It was little things, like body language, and statements like 'Not another boring training!'" said Ann, that indicated to her that staff was resistant to submitting to an outside trainer. However, she made her case to the executive sales director, who agreed that it was worth a try.

When Andy showed up with statistics about the upcoming target show, it demonstrated to Ann that Andy was well prepared. When they went through a three-hour training session that walked them through various scenarios, it was unanimous that the time was well spent.

"I really didn't think we'd get much out of it, but I was wrong," was one comment passed on to Ann. It was obvious to the staff that the training was beneficial for many reasons. On the tradeshow floor a month later,

"I found that almost the entire staff was more alert and practicing the techniques Andy had given us, specifically standing on the edge and being friendly and open, but not ready to pounce. There was a definite improvement," said Ann.

Booth staff training is a critical piece of the overall tradeshow marketing effort, and Ann's example is one of many that underscore the critical nature of using all tools at your disposal.

Knowledge Base

One element that may be important enough to insert into a training session is educating your employees on your company's goals and increasing their knowledge of your tradeshow marketing efforts. When employees are fully educated about the company's tradeshow marketing goals, they're more likely to buy in to the overall effort, which makes them more valuable.

Increasing the knowledge base of your employees is one of the best things you can do for your marketing efforts (tradeshow and otherwise). By knowing such things and more, the knowledge base increases and the company's connections grow, thereby increasing the buy-in on any company activity, including tradeshow marketing.

Loyalty and performance—they really work.

In the long term, increasing your employees' knowledge base equips and empowers those employees to represent the company, leading to improved interaction with attendees and increased results.

At Rooibee Red Tea, deciding which staff members to send to the Natural Products Expo West comes down to "who do we want to be in front of the buyer and decision makers?" That means the CEO, operations director, finance director, sales director, and other key people all attend, according to Zachary Anderson, creative director. There also needs to be someone present who knows all of the products well, from A to Z, and who can facilitate all of the necessary sampling of the teas in the booth.

"Telling the story" is a key element of any brand. Rooibee Red Tea wants the staff to both fully understand the story and how that story helps potential buyers understand its products.

Step Six Challenge

In section one of this challenge, determine if your average staffer knows the following:

Tradeshow Knowledge

1. Which shows do you exhibit at each year?
2. Which shows did you used to attend, but haven't for years?
3. Which shows are you considering exhibiting at, but haven't yet done so?
4. What's your potential audience at each show?
5. What's the potential audience for all shows for the whole year?
6. How many leads do you bring home from each show?

7. How many of those leads are actually followed up on?
8. How does the booth go together?
9. Who takes care of the shipping?
10. Who determines the marketing messaging and the main products promoted at each show?
11. What are the most important goals at each show?
12. How much money is budgeted for each show?
13. How much money is actually spent on the show?
14. Who takes care of the graphics printing?
15. What company builds the booth?
16. Where is the booth stored?
17. Where are the records of previous tradeshows kept, and who has access to those records?
18. How much business can you directly attribute to the leads gathered from the shows?
19. What's the return on investment on the sales leads you gathered from the shows?
20. Can you identify other show benefits that, while they don't directly impact your bottom line, are still valuable, such as branding, earned media mentions, gaining new distributors, or strengthening ties with current distributors?

Next, find out how much staffers know overall about the company.

Company Knowledge

1. How much do you know about the products and services the company produces?
2. Where are the company's products made?
3. Who designs them?
4. Who's in charge of what?
5. How many employees are there?

6. How many locations are there?
7. How familiar are you with the various team members?
8. How well do you know your boss? Is he or she married? Does he or she own a cat, drink coffee, have kids (and if so, how many)?

WHAT DO I DO WITH ALL OF THESE PEOPLE IN THE BOOTH?

How important are visitors?

As a tradeshow exhibitor, you want visitors—*lots* of them! The more the merrier. But how important are they, really? Can you put a value on each visitor to your company?

Let's say you've got a good plan for dealing with all of those visitors. You've been drawing people to the booth, your products are top notch, your staffers are well trained, and they know how to qualify and disqualify visitors and capture pertinent information.

So what's missing?

Ponder this: How much do you really know about the metrics of your visitors? Have you counted them? Have you identified the important ones?

Along with booth staff training (last step), tracking visitors to your booth on a show-by-show basis is probably the most overlooked facet of tradeshow marketing. However, if you can capture even a partial picture of the visitors to your booth, chances are you'll learn a lot and wonder why you didn't do this before.

Assembling the numbers and explaining them to the executive team may justify a program's existence. So, if that's the situation at your company, start digging. Take surveys, track overall impressions, track sales-lead potential, create sales histories, and collect as much information as possible. This research will allow you to put a quantifiable number on the cost of each impression at a tradeshow. Track the number of visitors, media mentions, sponsorship and promotion costs, and more. Done effectively, this is often an eye-opening experience for both the tradeshow marketing department and upper management.

Having real numbers will roll back the covers on what's really going on. In many cases, tradeshow marketing is one of the lowest cost-per-lead sales and marketing expenses.

No surprise there. However, you've still got to run the numbers to know for sure.

Here are some things to ask about your company's tradeshow marketing efforts:

- How many visitors do you get in your booth during each show?
- If you haven't ever measured that number, what are your best guesses?
- How many of the visitors are actual leads?

- How many of the leads are A (hot and need to be followed up on immediately)?
- How many of the leads are B (lukewarm—they will likely buy in the next six to twelve months)?
- How many of the leads are C (interested, but not ready to buy in the foreseeable future)?

If you have been tracking the visitor count year after year, you'll have an idea of the trends, along with the value of each visitor. This, of course, is valuable information that can provide insight into how your company is both performing at the shows and how the show itself is doing. The visitor count is a reflection of both your company's products and marketing effort, and the show's overall attendance and promotion.

More information about lead generation and lead tracking appears in step ten. For now, let's focus on the actual visitor metrics, which are still valuable even without tracking the leads.

If you're not tracking the visitor count and grading the leads, why not? Chances are, if you answer *no*, it's a manpower issue. After all, it's a big task to count those visitors.

However, if one person is tasked with that chore every hour (or half a day, or before lunch, or however you break it up), then another person takes over for the next shift, a picture of your overall booth attendance will begin to emerge—for starters.

Katie, our fictional exhibitor and marketing director from steps one and four, felt that she was on a steep learning curve when it came to finding ways to track all numbers and slice and dice the metrics once assembled.

"We have four to five staffers who rotate in and out of the booth through our show schedule, and while each of them can share their feelings, I've come to realize that the information is more anecdotal than anything and not necessarily useful," said Katie.

"Too often, huge financial decisions are made on what a group of salespeople's anecdotal feedback is about a particular show," I said. "If a salesperson feels that people are in a buying mood at one show, your company might keep that show on the schedule. If they feel another show doesn't have the same *buying vibe*, the show might be dropped. They might be right, but they could be wrong. But you won't know unless you run the numbers."

"Exactly. So while we were very busy during the show, we felt it was important to do our best to track the numbers," said Katie. "We had a clipboard with a pen on a string, right under the front greeting counter, and we'd track everything. We put a mark for everyone who stopped and took a bite, we had another column for people who stopped and talked to us, and a third column for people we actually had sit-down meetings with, whether they were scheduled previously or if they just happened randomly. And of course we counted every single cookie sample we handed out."

Visitors in your booth are a great opportunity to gather current market information through surveys.

While attending the Outdoor Retailer industry show in Salt Lake City, I checked out Twitter for the latest tweets using the #ORShow hashtag and noticed that a sock seller was giving away free socks to the first one hundred visitors of the day. Always up for free socks, I stopped by the booth early.

The socks were free—almost. I had to spend about three or four minutes in front of an iPad answering survey questions that asked me all sorts of things having to do with sock usage, types of socks I like and purchase, along with some demographic information. I was glad to give them the info in exchange for the socks.

What information you can gather from visitors depends on what's important to you at that show. Are you interested in finding out which products caught their eye? Are you interested in their reactions to your new exhibit? Perhaps you'd like to know what they don't like about your products.

The fact is, when you have thousands of visitors, it almost seems a crime not to take advantage of the opportunity to ask questions—a lot of them. Don't push it, of course, and don't ask someone who is not interested in sharing a few moments. But with those who are interested, take advantage of it.

Below are various visitor elements you might track:

Exit Survey: Talk to between twenty-five and two hundred visitors and query them with a short survey. While you can ask many close-ended questions requiring only a *yes* or *no*, be sure to include a couple of open-ended questions to give visitors a chance to expound on an item.

Preshow and Postshow Awareness Survey: This is a good way to gauge visitors' before-and-after brand awareness at a tradeshow. Before the doors open, ask those waiting to get in what they know about your brand with a sample question or two. After the show, ask visitors the same set of questions as they exit.

Self-Survey: Ask in-booth visitors to spend a few moments on an iPad answering questions. Offer an incentive of a small gift or the chance to win a larger prize if they provide contact information and rate their level of interest in your products or services.

While most companies have the ability to do all of the above metric measurements in-house, it might make sense to outsource the last item.

Qualitative Analysis: Hire a professional survey company to look closely into branding and awareness issues, such as brand impressions, visual reach, audience interest, customer journeys, and more.

Now that you have numbers, what do they mean?

Step Seven Challenge

Answer and discuss the following questions with your team:

1. What questions do visitors ask most about your products? Now that you have someone making a mark on a clipboard for every booth visitor, next have him or her record any questions that visitors ask about your products. Not only will this task keep that

person busy, but it will also provide insight into what people are thinking about when it comes to your products or services.

2. How many in-booth meetings are pre-scheduled?
3. How many meetings happen because a potential client dropped by the booth?
4. How many people attend those meetings?
5. Who is in the meeting?
6. Do you have enough space for all the meetings, both scheduled and unscheduled, during the show?
7. If you don't have enough space in the booth for meetings, how are you addressing that? Are you adding more meeting space, tables, and chairs, and crowding the other tables? Or are you finding off-site space for meetings?

We'll cover professional presentations extensively in step twelve. For the time being, let's consider the metrics of in-booth demonstrations.

If your company offers product demonstrations in the booth, you should track these metrics:

1. How many demonstrations were given during the show?
2. How many visitors attended those demonstrations?
3. What was the average attendance per demonstration?
4. What time(s) of day is/are best at a particular show for demonstrations?
5. How many leads were developed over the course of the demonstrations?
6. Which presenters attract the best audiences?
7. Which products or services translate best to presentations?
8. What is the closing ratio of the leads gathered as a result of your demonstrations?

The net result of all of this tracking is to give you the ability to break down costs and visitor impact and track trends in your booth across shows.

TWEETING, POSTING, AND INSTAGRAMMING LIKE A KING OR QUEEN

Having written, blogged, spoken, and taught social media in conjunction with events, conferences, and tradeshows, I would be remiss if I didn't include a step or two on that topic. My blog at TradeshowguyBlog.com is chock-full of hundreds of articles, including case studies, examples, and lists of things to do with social media to drive traffic, move people around, and engage tradeshow goers.

It's a big subject that deserves its own book (which I actually wrote, self-published, and handed out in early 2014), so it can't be fully explained in one step. Nevertheless, we can establish the following:

- Social media is used by many, if not all, of your competitors.
- Many companies don't use social media properly, or get lost when trying to navigate the ins and outs—and many of them are still not getting out of the starting gate.
- Your audience *is definitely* engaged in social media.

Why Not Social Media?

If you get only one thing out of this step, remember this: There is no one way to effectively engage in social media. Each company has a different level of knowledge and resources available. Whatever the level of engagement at yours, you'll find some competitors doing it better and others doing it worse.

If you're not using social media, why not?

A few years ago, my business partner Roger and I were hired to do research for a large multinational company involved in the heavy metals industry (think titanium, not Metallica). The marketing director made it clear that the company's management had no interest in and would never get involved in social media.

The company's management felt that social media was, in their words, kid stuff, and any adult caught at their company spending time on social media was wasting time—theirs and the company's. It didn't matter that their competitors were using social media. It was *verboten*—a wasteland, not to be discussed or considered. It was, actually, to be laughed at.

The marketing director, Kirk, felt otherwise. Fortunately, though he was hamstrung by management, he did manage to come up with a budget for us to "listen" to social media for an ongoing project.

We set up a listening post, using a premium dashboard tool allowing us to track traffic relating to a handful of keywords through millions of blogs, tweets, and news stories. We also set up Google Alerts on the same keywords and then sat back and watched the information flow.

It took a while to refine the keywords, perhaps three to five weeks, before we were getting good information on products, competitors, and industry chat.

After about three months, we realized a few things:

- There was definitely online chatter relating to heavy metals in the industry.
- Most of the engineers in the heavy metal industry hung out on Twitter, frequently trading links and information.
- We discovered we really didn't need the expensive, premium dashboard we had leased. So we dropped it.

We'd regularly e-mail and meet with Kirk to show him what we found. Often, we had information that was shared online before it came to him through normal channels. Occasionally, we'd come up with a nugget of information that put him in the catbird seat and made him look good. A couple of times, people asked him where he had found that information.

The project clearly showed us that in spite of his management's head-in-the-sand approach, the heavy metals industry was heavily engaged in social media, regularly exchanging valuable information. It's a pretty sure bet that your industry is heavily involved, too.

Listening to Social Media

If someone told you that you could listen to the online conversations of your prospects, customers, stakeholders, competitors, and employees, would you? Yes, you would. It's critical to success in today's online world. Listening is important. In fact, if nothing else, you'll learn by listening and watching your industry.

Set up Google Alerts for daily search summaries. Track and search hashtags on Twitter. Look for information about competitors, products (yours and your competitors'), track management of other companies (don't you think they're not tracking you), and generally be a snoop online. The information is there, and if you're not tracking it, I can guarantee you that many of your competitors are tracking you—closely.

By tracking your industry on social media, you are better equipped to engage with your key audiences in a genuine way.

There are many free tools to track conversations online. In fact, searching Twitter for hashtags, keywords, and phrases can give you a quick insight into current thoughts and discussions. If you're unfamiliar with hashtags, just put a "#" in front of a word or amalgamation of words and there's your hashtag. "#ExpoWest" is the hashtag used regularly for the Natural Products Expo West show. "#Eventprofs" is a hashtag used in conjunction with event professionals.

Twitter and Instagram have made hashtag links "hot," which means by clicking on them, you'll open up a search page with hashtag-related results. Performing a Google Blog Search at Google.com/blogsearch can narrow down your search from every indexed web page to just the blogs. Check out BlogSearchEngine.com, Alltop.com, Technorati.com, Guzzle.it, and others. Books get outdated, but Google, Bing, and other search engines keep the most-active and up-to-date search results on their first page or two.

You can also consider the following listening tools in building your own social media listening platform:

- Ice Rocket
- How Social
- Klout
- Twitter Counter
- Facebook Search
- ???—By the time you read this, all of the above may be in the deep dustbin on Internet history. So just search for "social media listening platform" and see what works for you.

Engagement

The real-time connectivity of social media has changed the world. Why would you *not* get involved? And don't say your industry is not involved. Every industry is.

And you can't say you're too old. Too lazy? Sure. But not too old. There are people older than you are who have found a way to use social media and are very adept at it.

And don't say you don't have time. There may be some truth to that, but even the busiest people find time to post thoughts, articles, photos, videos, and read and respond to the same from others.

So, where to start?

As a business—and especially as a business looking to focus on using social media for event and tradeshow marketing—spend time identifying your *objectives*, just like you do with your other marketing endeavors.

What do you want to accomplish with your social media engagement at shows? If all you want are sales, you'll be disappointed, because social media doesn't really drive sales at tradeshows. However, it can and does drive people to move from one location to another.

If you are hoping to find new ways to engage your market, to discover their likes and dislikes, identify complaints or answer questions, or solve problems, then social media is built for you. In fact, if some genius mad scientist decided to invent a way to help connect the thousands of trade-show attendees via digital media, he couldn't do a better job than inventing all the social media platforms we have at our beck and call.

When it comes to using social media at events, you'll want to know some obvious ways to use it. OK, that's easy. Use it to drive traffic to your booth, to promote products and services, to make connections with your audience, fans, and colleagues. The key is to make it *fun* and keep it light. Social media, at least for companies, is not a place to make heavy political statements or slam competitors. Not that a little levity at your competitors' expense doesn't have its place, but it should be done strategically.

Next, you must identify *who* is going to represent your company. Is it your marketing team? A senior exec? An outside agency? All three?

Often, a combination works best. Your employees know your company culture, which is important in striking the right tone in posts and keeping important information at the forefront. An experienced agency, on the other hand, knows the pitfalls of tweeting inappropriately or responding to a sudden social media crisis.

Next, determine the best social media *platforms*. While there are several key platforms that come to mind—Facebook, Twitter, YouTube, Instagram, Pinterest—it often takes an experienced agency to identify the most important ones. Basically, the ones where your target market hangs out and engages the most are key. If you're currently involved in a handful of platforms, you probably have an intuitive understanding of the ones your audience responds to best.

Finally, you have to create *content*, and it must be created continuously and consistently. How many Twitter or Facebook accounts have you seen that are dormant, where the last post was over a year ago? It happens all the time. This goes back to identifying the resources you have available, either in-house or provided by an agency.

Content comes in many forms: tweets, blog posts, short Facebook posts, photos, videos, and responses to comments and questions on your platforms. When you get involved in social media, you must make a commitment, and that commitment extends beyond the next month or year.

Social media is a marketing initiative, but unlike other marketing initiatives, there is no end date. An advertising campaign has a stop and start date. Social media is ongoing, and the commitment is ongoing, too.

Knowing that you must be committed shouldn't keep you from getting involved. If nothing else, pick a platform—Facebook is probably the obvious choice if you're not already there—create an account, and start.

That's all it takes to begin. You can make adjustments and learn as you go. That's what your competitors are doing.

When it comes to using social media at tradeshows, there's a *lot* more to discuss. This is why I'm giving you a PDF copy of my latest book, *Super Networking at Events and Tradeshows Using Social Media*. Find the link at the back of the book.

Step Eight Challenge

Answer the following questions, and discuss them with your marketing team:

1. Do you actively engage in social media to promote your tradeshow appearances?
2. Do you have a dedicated social media staffer attending shows?
3. If not, do you hire a third party? If so, how does that work?
4. How are social media postings shared with your staff?
5. How effectively do your social media staffers post valuable and interesting content?
6. Do you run any contests on social media to drive booth traffic? Discuss how they worked or didn't work.
7. Which social media platforms does your company use? Which are the most popular? Detail any metrics that you have available.
8. Are there any platforms that you think you should be on, but are not?

WHO'S KEEPING TRACK OF THOSE DAMN TWEETS?

Content creation, frankly, is fun. Or it's a pain in the ass, depending on your point of view. It's potentially the most challenging part of getting involved and engaged with social media.

When presented with the challenge of creating content, people not used to creating content on a regular basis will often see it as a stressful activity because they don't know what to create. Let's look at some ways to remove this anxiety and have a little fun.

What kind of content are you able to create? Simple. You've got options for writing or creating multimedia such as photographs, videos, and audio. These show up as photos, blog posts, videos, tweets, Facebook posts, Google+ posts, podcasts, and more.

Where will this content be disseminated?

How often should we create content?

And finally, *who* is going to create it?

If we shoot video, for instance, should we worry about hiring a professional videographer and editor so the videos are top notch and high quality, or does that really matter?

If you're posting photos, who's going to take them?

Who's in charge, anyway? Let's explore this topic further. And if you tense up at all of the potential outlets you have to take on, take a deep breath. Don't worry. I won't ask you to do more than you're up to at any given moment.

Wally, the Pharaoh head of business development, doesn't tweet. He doesn't Facebook, doesn't Google, doesn't Instagram, and definitely doesn't Vine. Although he has a smartphone, he uses it mostly for phone calls, texting, reading news and books, and checking sports scores. We're still waiting for him to sign up for a LinkedIn account. However, that doesn't mean he discounts the value of social media.

"We have a small team, actually three people, that take turns providing content for all of our social media outlets," said Wally.

"What is your main goal with social media?" I asked.

"We realize that no matter how good or bad we are, there will be companies that do it better and those that do it worse than us. We can have a great, consistent presence on several platforms and still not do what some of our competitors are doing.

"The main thing is to make sure we are accurately reading our audience," Wally added.

"What do you mean by that?"

"It means that we track comments on our platforms, respond when appropriate, and look for any problems that may crop up, such as negative comments or reviews. We don't try and prevent them, but instead feel that negative comments, which we don't get all that much, are a good opportunity to learn and correct any issues surrounding our products. We realize we're not perfect."

"Agreed," I responded. "So what kind of content are you producing, and how is it done?"

"Because we're a pretty large privately held company that sells to millions of consumers, we don't have a blog, although that's been a bit of an ongoing conversation for years. In the early days of blogs, back around 2005, we didn't want to be the first because we wanted to see how they went. And once social media started to grow, we got onto Facebook, and eventually Twitter and Instagram," said Wally.

"As to your question about who creates it, we have always worked with a local photo studio that keeps us supplied with photos of our products and goodies that can be made from them. It's a combination of studio shots and curated images from our events."

"Events?" I asked. "Does that mean you plan on making photos available on your social media platforms from tradeshows?"

"Not necessarily tradeshows, but more customer-oriented events where we have a lot of people having fun and enjoying our goodies. The marketing team is always taking photos of people enjoying our goodies. And we make sure to get permission from the people in the images, either in writing or verbally on video. We know that hundreds of thousands of people can see the photos, so we do our due diligence on that," said Wally.

"Let me go back to something you said a moment ago. Why don't you have a blog now, because so many companies think that it's such a good thing? It's a valuable piece of real estate to so many people," I said.

"We had many discussions about the possibility of a blog. And yes, it is valuable to many companies. But the things that helped us decide not to start a blog had to do with who would create the content at the time, and by the time we had those people in place, the social media platforms made so much sense for us. Also, the fact that we sell to consumers means that a blog isn't really the big deal that it might be to a B2B [business-to-business] company," said Wally.

One key to consistently creating good, usable content is always to have that goal in the back of your mind. Always be thinking about what you can photograph, what you can blog about, or what might make a nice short video.

Let's return to a previous observation: There will be some companies that do it better and some that do it worse. No matter what, you'll fall somewhere in the middle.

Back to the *what* part of our earlier stress-test quiz.

The main types of social media content are blog posts, photos, videos, and tweets. That's it. Everything will pretty much fall under those four categories. At least until an exciting new social media tool or platform supersedes them.

Blogging

Blog posts can answer questions, promote new products, and help readers solve problems, and may include multimedia such as videos, photos, or audio (podcasting). If you don't have an active blog, you're missing out on the most valuable piece of online real estate a company can have.

If you're serious about blogging for your business, find a good corporate blogging book and digest it from front to back. Debbie Weil, for instance, has written books on corporate blogging that are worth your time.

In the meantime, let's review the benefits and dangers of blogging.

First and foremost, your blog is not a place for your company to regularly toot its own horn. When you land on a company blog and see blog posts that tout its new products, or a post about the CEO visiting some exotic foreign locale to pal around with muckety-mucks or bragging about some award it won, do you really care? Is there anything there that inspires you to spend more than a few seconds on that site? Not likely.

On the other hand, as a reader, if the blog addresses your business challenges, helps you solve problems, warns you what things to avoid, gives you new ideas to help build your business, and truly provides information that helps transform your thinking and even your business, wouldn't you want to visit that blog again and again?

Naturally. It becomes a valuable resource. But a blog that brags about how cool of a company it is? Not so much. As a blogger, you'd be much better off keeping your eyes and ears on the challenges your customers face, and help them to solve those challenges.

Writing Makes You a Better Writer

Regularly committing your thoughts to a public blog forces you to think. Researching and writing will force you to become better educated and well informed about those issues. When you run across a problem your readers have that you don't know how to solve, you'll be pressed to find an answer. That may mean digging deeper or making contact with an industry expert or consultant and getting his or her advice.

If you become a dedicated blogger, you'll spend time meeting and talking to industry consultants and experts, along with clients and prospects, all to help answer the questions that arise as a result of your blogging.

You'll become a better writer. You'll be better informed. You'll gain at least a little notoriety. And if you continue to write good material that helps to solve the problems your market faces, you'll likely become an (gasp!) *expert* in the field.

And being an expert usually leads people to seek you out and want to buy your products or services. All because you're the expert, the go-to guy or girl in the industry.

Videos

It used to be that you had to spend thousands of dollars to hire a video production team if you wanted any sort of decent-quality video to represent your company. Then came small and inexpensive video cameras, such as the Flip camera and similar products, allowing easy creation of videos. These don't quite reach the quality of hiring a professional videographer, but with tens of thousands of companies posting videos, it doesn't take much to create a video of modest quality to demonstrate how a product works or show a customer talking about how your product helped solve his or her problem. The quality of amateur video improved, and the value of high-quality production decreased.

Along came smartphones such as the iPhone, and Flip video cameras vanished. With the explosion of social media and smartphones, it's a simple matter to shoot and edit a short video and upload it to the Internet in minutes.

Soon, companies were commonly showing potential audiences online how their products worked (search for "Will it blend?" on YouTube to see what Blendtec does to promote their line of high-quality blenders) or what their customers thought about their products.

On the flip side, social media allowed people to complain far and wide when a company dropped the ball in dealing with its customers. Search YouTube for "United Breaks Guitars" for what one passenger thought about United Airlines' failure in dealing with him when they broke his guitar. Long story short: United Airlines got a ton of bad press, had no ability (or interest) in responding to the negative social media avalanche, and when they finally did realize what was happening, they struggled with how to deal with being buried in the online negativity.

Videos can be powerful. YouTube is the second largest search engine online, behind Google. It probably hasn't escaped you that Google owns YouTube and incorporates YouTube videos into Google search results. If you have a popular video on YouTube, it can be found on both YouTube and Google as well as other search engines.

A good friend of mine is a former auto body shop owner. He's posted a few dozen videos online that explain some of the finer points of auto body painting and repair, attracting hundreds of thousands of views.

Videos are cool. Videos are attractive. Videos can show how things work much better than simply writing about it. Videos have personality. Videos can go viral.

Are you shooting and posting videos on your YouTube channel on a regular basis? Do you even have your own YouTube channel? It takes only a few moments to set up, and it provides a platform to show off skills, personality, and insights into addressing and solving problems in your industry. It's one more way you can become recognized as an expert.

Photos

More than two-thirds of all Americans carry a smartphone, which means that most people have a high-definition camera in their pocket or purse at all times.

Photos can be used as effectively as video, and sometimes more effectively. Snapshots of company employees, clients, products, and demos can be spread throughout the social media ecosphere in a short time. Photos can be posted on Twitter, Facebook, Instagram, Google+, and more.

If your company makes products for outdoor use, invite users to post photos of that product in action outdoors. They'll post photos depicting situations that you could never dream up if you had hired ten top photographers (same is true of videos).

Do you have a cool factory? By opening the doors to your factory with the use of photos and video, you lift the veil on processes that previously may have been a mystery to your fans and followers.

Do you have a visitor in your booth raving about your product? Shoot a still photo or a video of him or her with the product.

Use photos on your blog as well as other social media outlets. It's all part of content creation.

Engaging with Tradeshow Attendees

As I mentioned earlier, if some mad scientist had designed the best way to use digital media to connect event visitors, he or she would have come up with social media. Social media and events fit like a hand in a glove.

So you're planning your tradeshow appearance, and a few weeks ahead of time you're told that your company will be previewing a new whiz-bang product at the show. They give you free rein to tell the world.

Hop on Twitter, Facebook, and YouTube to promote that new whiz-bang product. You use the show hashtag to make sure that anyone searching for show information on Twitter or Facebook can find your tweet or post:

#Expowest is where we'll release the new Choco-Chip M&M cookie! Check us out at booth 4567!

See? You used the hashtag that all show attendees who engage with Twitter know. You mentioned both the booth number and the new product.

Chances are that several show exhibitors and attendees will see it and retweet it to their followers. So instead of just your followers having a chance to see it, the announcement has been spread a little further.

On the next day, take a photo of the cookie, and post it on Facebook and Twitter, with the hashtag, company name, and booth number. Again, you'll see retweets and salivating audience members who can't wait to bite into your new cookie.

Then, a day or two later, shoot a brief video—perhaps fifteen seconds or shorter—of your cookie creator pulling a batch of new cookies out of the oven, biting into one, and saying "*Yes!*" Post it on YouTube, Twitter, Facebook, and Instagram, again mentioning the booth number, using the show hashtag, and citing your company name.

Because your audience has seen the first announcement, and then the photo, and now the video, your content will be shared even more.

And you're not even at the show yet. Just wait until you start handing out those cookies.

Finally, send out a tweet the day before the show that goes something like this:

#Expowest Come by booth 4567 for the new Choco-Chip M&M cookie. The first fifty receive a free T-shirt! Doors open at ten Friday!

Expect a rush!

Other Types of Content

Here are other types of content that you might consider for your blog or social media efforts.

Infographics: You've seen these even, perhaps without recognizing exactly what they are. Infographics are clever graphics that explain information using graphs, illustrations, and text. Explaining a complicated subject visually gives you a better chance of getting people to read about and understand it in the first place. Infographics are also the type of content that gets shared again and again through social media.

How do you create infographics? I used to think that I needed killer Photoshop or illustration skills or the ability to pay someone thousands of dollars, but that's not the case. There are several infographic-creation websites and tools online, and many of them have both free and premium versions. Check out Pikotochart.com, Infogr.am, Create.visual.ly, or just search for "create infographics" and you'll find a list of current websites that can walk you through the process.

Memes: You've seen these, too, but probably haven't known exactly what to call them. They're iconic photos, usually from movies or TV shows, that have cute little sayings. Check out samples and create your own by searching for "meme generator."

Generally speaking, memes are usually reserved for sharing on social media, and not for use on your blog. They're too cute, quickly digested, and have such a short shelf life that putting them on a blog doesn't make much sense. But social media? Sure.

Book Reviews: Self-descriptive. Read a book that people within your industry may like to learn about. Write a brief review and put it on your blog.

How-tos and Guides: These can be short-, medium-, or long-content pieces. If you want to create a longer piece such as a detailed guide, consider hiring an illustrator and designer. Often, these pieces are created and saved as PDFs, which can be downloaded, either with a direct link on your blog or through a "squeeze" page that squeezes a visitor's contact information in exchange for access.

How-tos can be quick demonstrations via text, graphics, or video that break down the steps on how something works.

Rants and/or Opinion Pieces: Feel something in your industry isn't working well? Or do you see something that you think should be changed? Take time to structure an opinion piece, much like you see in the opinion section of your newspaper.

Keep in mind that a controversial opinion piece will get shared online more often than a typical blog piece. Be humble, don't just rant for the sake of ranting, keep it civil, and encourage dissenting opinions.

Opinion pieces shouldn't be a regular thing, but instead should be mixed in occasionally with other types of content—unless, of course, your personality and writing style are very opinionated, and that's what people tend to know you for.

Lists: People love lists. From my experience, they are the most-read and most-shared types of blog posts. Start writing a list, and when you're done, you have a number. That's how I wrote my first tradeshow e-book, *101 Rules of Tradeshow Marketing*. (See download link in the back of the book.)

Product Reviews: While this can be a review of your company's products, you'll likely get more mileage out of reviewing products that work well *with* your products, or that may somehow assist your target audience, whether related to your products or not.

Interviews: Interviews and transcriptions with industry professionals, consultants, or experts represent one method; you might also consider recording such conversations if you have the ability to post audio files as podcasts. Failing that, you might want to post an edited transcript of the interview. Be sure to include a photo of your interview subject and a link back to his or her blog, Twitter account, Facebook page, or whatever else they'd like.

Podcasts: Speaking of podcasting, if you're the kind of person who is better sitting in front of a microphone and just ad-libbing your viewpoint, perhaps a podcast makes sense. They're easy to produce and post. All you really need is a microphone and audio recording software, and you can do them virtually anywhere with a desktop, laptop, or even a smartphone.

Case Studies: Have a client with a great story to tell? Case studies are readable and sharable content because people love to learn about what worked for others and how it worked.

You can structure a case study in many ways, but if you present the challenges, the solution, and the many twists and turns along the way, that makes for an informative and entertaining read.

E-books: E-books are longer pieces, but they don't have to be the length of regular books. The *101 Rules of Tradeshow Marketing* tome was simply that: 101 rules. Each rule was just a sentence or two, and the whole thing came to fewer than thirty pages.

To make the book more attractive, hire a pro to assemble a creative layout and design. Whether you give it away free with no strings attached, or put it behind a gated page that asks for a name and e-mail address, include your contact information in the e-book.

Research: I once posted a brief, two-question survey on SurveyMonkey.com and asked people to take a few seconds and quickly answer the questions. I wanted to get a little anecdotal, informal information to uncover what people were thinking regarding their biggest challenge in tradeshow marketing, but I knew I'd get a brief blog post out of it, too.

The research can be as quick as a short online survey or as in-depth and detailed as hiring a research firm to make hundreds or thousands of phone calls. Whatever the case, if you create the information, it belongs to you and you can use it in any way you'd like.

If the information has high value, you may consider writing an in-depth report and offering it for sale. In that case, create both a free summary and a blog post to share it. You might also consider creating an infographic based on the content, which is easily digestible and shareable.

Other types of social media content might include the following:

Questions and Conversations: Ask people what they think, what they feel, and how they use a given product. Cite anecdotes, answer questions, offer ideas.

Funny Content: OK, not everybody is funny and, in fact, humor is usually hard to do. If you really want to know how hard it is to create consistent comedy, read Steve Martin's *Born Standing Up* and you'll see the path he followed as he learned stand-up comedy. In most cases, it should be left to professionals. However, that shouldn't stop you if something funny and innocuous comes to mind. When it comes to humor online—and especially when you're representing your brand—keep it clean, use it sparingly, and try to find some connection between the humor and your products or services.

Promotional Content: Quick question: What's the fastest way to lose followers and subscribers? Pummel them with promotions! But if you've spent time sharing good information, providing answers to questions, and becoming an expert, your readers will be more receptive when you throw a promo their way. And if you can find a way to make the promotion fun, all the better. A photo contest, for example, may encourage your audience to share personal photos using your products. In such cases, your audience is actually promoting your business and products for you. Offer a chance to win a prize for their participation so they feel engaged.

Still, promotional content should be used sparingly. Use the old 80/20 rule: For every four informational and educational posts, feel free to post something promotional. Most blogs are more like 10:1 or 20:1, but no matter your actual ratio, you should lean heavily away from anything but a whiff of promotion.

When it comes to content creation, there are literally dozens of ways you can create content and package it for your blog or social media outlets. And of course when you do create content for your blog, make sure you share that blog post throughout your social media ecosphere, posting links to grab as many click-throughs and readers as possible.

Step Nine Challenge

Discuss the following with your staff:

1. Does your company have a dedicated blogger? Photographer? Videographer?
2. How are those various pieces of content used?
3. Do you have a blog or other platform (social media) to share those pieces of content?
4. Do you use photos or videos from one show throughout the year?
5. How many photos and videos did you take at the last show?
6. Do you plan to shoot more or less video at the next show?

GOT A STACK OF LEADS: NOW WHAT?

B efore jumping into lead generation, let's define what it is and isn't.

Lead generation is *not* putting out a fishbowl for visitors to drop in a business card for a chance to win an iPad or a steak dinner. It is *not* the act of having people line up to spin a prize wheel.

Lead generation *is* an activity designed to capture information from qualified buyers.

At tradeshows, lead generation is the specific act of determining a visitor's qualifications for buying and capturing contact and related information so you can connect with them again in the not-too-distant future.

Lead generation begins long before the show. Not that the show isn't important, but it's just the staged part of an entire process that begins early and continues long after the show concludes.

Starting Your Lead-Generation Process

As a tradeshow marketer, you have numerous opportunities to engage with a potential client. You should be coming up with a couple of dozen ways to "touch" them before, during, and after the show. One way to reach out to potential clients before the show is to invest in an e-mail blast to attendees, inviting them to watch a short video that teaches them how to do something, solve a problem, achieve a goal, or satisfy a need.

Let's go back to Wally, our fictional head of business development for Pharaoh.

"What is Pharaoh's process for 'touching' business partners, distributors, and potential clients?"

"At our most recent show, we sent out an e-mail to attendees, with an invitation asking them to watch a short video entitled *How to Increase Sales with Grocery Store Selling Sections, Top to Bottom.* The video was about two minutes long and was targeted at grocery retailers, showing them how a larger 'sell' section would increase sales of their products," Wally explained.

"Later, during the show, attendees were invited to register for a webinar that walked them through the value of pitching non-GMO and gluten-free products. If an attendee registered for the webinar, his or her name went into the hot and qualified lead list. For the next eight weeks, those potential clients would receive another automated e-mail and at least two phone calls from salespeople. Each of the e-mails would lead to another video, white paper, webinar, or other educational nonsales pieces that would position Pharaoh as the go-to company for grains and related products. Once someone became a client, he or she would then receive regular support, including calls, e-mails leading to more videos, and educational pieces positioned to support the customer in the quest to sell more products."

Wally detailed the lead-generation process, saying it's geared to take advantage of all of the methods of communication available, including e-mail, snail mail such as postcards and other mailed items, phone calls, and more. Communication is regular and consistent, touching potential clients several times before, during, and after the tradeshow.

Information offered to potential clients should be directly related to problems that they regularly run into, helping to solve a problem, satisfy a need, or achieve a goal. Your visitor is looking to solve problems, and if your company's products and services are seen as a part of the solution, the person will be more receptive to your sales proposition.

Qualifying or Disqualifying a Visitor

At your booth, you'll get lots of visitors. Before spending valuable floor time with them, you need to qualify them.

Persons are qualified if they represent a company (or themselves) as interested in your products or services, and they are in a position to consider buying something from you in the near future. If you're at a tradeshow to sign up distributors, those people must be representing a company, such as a store or chain of stores, that is looking for new products to sell.

When visitors enter your booth, they are expressing a desire to learn more about your products. You now have an opportunity to learn a few things about them: who they are, the type of interest they have, and whether they are in a position to purchase soon.

As they enter your booth, assuming your graphic messaging is correct (see step five), the booth will have already qualified or disqualified visitors. In short, those graphics are laser focused on your products and services and their benefits.

That messaging might mean a specific statement, a bold claim, or a question that causes visitors to think, "Hey, I need to know more!" If your graphics are successful, show attendees walking the floor will enter your booth.

Let's bring in Katie, our fictional marketing director from Gotcha! Cookies 'n' Treats, and see what she's up against.

One of Katie's primary goals is to develop a bigger network of distributors in her company's region. So, if visitor Bob comes by the booth and says his company loves the cookies, but he's from the other side of the country, does that make his distributorship a qualified prospect? No, it is too far away, and the cookies will take too long to ship at a reasonable cost.

That doesn't mean that Katie should dismiss Bob out of hand. He may be a future prospect when overnight shipping becomes feasible or Katie's company expands into Bob's territory. Or Bob may know someone who represents a company closer to home. So Katie spends time asking questions.

Based on that conversation, she has determined the information she needs and when or if to follow up with Bob.

Collecting Information and Inviting Further Engagement

Once you've qualified a visitor, what is the minimum information needed to move to the next step?

In sales, agreeing with your prospect on the next step is critical before the current meeting or phone call is over. No matter what you're doing, the final thing before disengaging is to agree on the next step.

At a tradeshow, once you've determined a need and a desire, it's time to move to the next steps—when to follow up and how to follow up.

Enter Lew Hoff of Bartizan, a company that has developed iLeads, lead-generation software that is essentially an app that resides on a smartphone or tablet.

According to Lew, "The great thing about having it on your smart-phone is that you can capture a lead anywhere. At tradeshows, you're not spending all of your time on the tradeshow floor. You can meet people at after-show parties, dinners, clubs, and so forth. If you find a real lead there, it's easy to capture the important information quickly and move on. And with the iLeads app, that information is automatically warehoused and shared back at the office."

Katie uses iLeads. She meets Jennifer at a postshow party and discovers that she represents a small store in her region. Although Jennifer isn't the final decision maker for her company, she does have strong influence.

"So, Jenny," said Katie, "what would you like for us to plan as the next step?"

"I'd like to have you ship a small sample package next week. John, the owner, will be in the office, and he would like to sample the cookies and see if they're a fit for our store," said Jenny.

"And when would be a good time to follow up?" Katie asked.

"I'd say in about three weeks. John will get the samples next week, but we won't review new products or make decisions until the end of the month," said Jenny.

Katie is entering this in her iLeads app while chatting at the after-show party. "OK, Jenny. I have you down for a sample package next week. What specifically are you interested in? The cookie line, or should we add in some of the treats line, like the chocolate rice crisp and peanut brittle?"

"Right now, let's start with the cookies. We'll want to sample them all eventually, but we're in the process of revamping our checkout counters to give us more space for more items and anything beyond the cookies would be in our way. Give us a couple of months on that," said Jenny.

"Sounds good," said Katie. "Let me confirm: samples of cookies next week, follow-up call with you in three weeks."

"Yes," said Jenny.

"OK, let me make sure I have your name spelled correctly, and your shipping address, phone number, and e-mail."

Before letting Jenny go, Katie confirmed the type of follow-up (shipping only cookies), when to follow up (three weeks), and who to call (Jenny). She also confirmed all of the necessary contact information. It's all from a playbook that should be familiar to any person who's gone through a Sales 101 class, and the steps can be easily accommodated in iLeads or a similar program or method.

Once that's done, Katie can move on. A brief encounter like this won't take much time. It's focused on the necessary elements and leaves out unnecessary material.

There are a hundred ways to attract a prospect, but they all boil down to this question: Are your products designed to solve a problem, satisfy a need, or achieve an objective? If so, are you able to communicate those propositions clearly to your audience? Then you're on the right track, and you will attract the right prospects.

If you have the resources and access to customer relationship management (CRM) automation, you should strongly consider using that method to stay in touch with potential clients (and new clients, too) via personalized postcards, online videos, links to special reports and white papers, and other educational, informational, and training materials.

As you move further into lead generation and nurturing, you'll want to rate each potential client with some rating system. Whether it's Hot, Warm, and Cool, or giving them a ranking from one to ten, your marketing follow-up system, be it automated or manually implemented, should stay in touch.

At Rooibee Red Tea (which we met in step five), postshow follow-up is critical to the company's success. With a huge influx of business cards at each show, it has to have a system to make sure that each contact is both classified and properly followed up on.

According to Rooibee Red Tea's creative director, Zachary Anderson, "We want to understand each contact, how we're going to follow up, how we're going to connect with them, and giving them a reason to want to remember us. We have to be really careful managing that interaction with each person."

Anderson describes how all company booth staffers have notebooks and how each one takes notes that relate to each business card and interaction. It's important for each person to go through the notebook as soon as the show is over, understand those interactions, and determine the next step. The immediate goal is to meet and connect with the buyer, but the end result is to get the consumer to want to sample the product, which is why the initial connection with the buyer is critical to taking the process to the next step.

"The thing that I'm most proud of is being able to connect one on one, and that people are allowed to not just experience our great products, but also to really buy into our story and growth potential," said Anderson. "It's not just what we have, but why we want to do it." That seems to be one critical area many tradeshow marketers miss.

Professional Presenters

Should you hire a professional presenter to increase the number of qualified leads?

Before you can make that determination, let's look at this from a few angles.

First, hiring a professional presenter will cost you. If he or she is really good, you'll be paying for expertise, experience, and personality. You'll have to pay for travel and lodging expenses as well, plus their fee for presenting at the tradeshow.

Next, do you have the space for a professional presenter and an audience?

Finally, does your product lend itself to using a professional presenter?

I posed those questions to Andy Saks of Spark Presentations and Ken Newman of Magnet Productions. Both have been doing professional trade-show presentations for clients for years, and they have seen exactly what it takes to draw a crowd and capture more leads. In other words, they're pros.

As Andy put it, "For most companies, the goal is to generate more leads and create potential sales. Not only that, but to get more qualified leads from people who have seen and understood the product. After sixteen years, I strongly believe that having a professional presenter is an ideal way to meet that goal.

"There are incredible efficiencies involved. First of all, you're attracting tons of people from the aisle. You're bringing them into the booth and setting them at ease using humor and entertainment. You're engaging them and telling them just enough about the product so that they want to know more, which is their incentive to stick around after the presentation and talk to the staff and see a demo and maybe give them a little prize or something," says Andy.

Andy explained that consistent demonstrations keep people circulating through the booth. Just do the math: A presenter can do two presentations of average length of 5-10 minutes an hour at minimum. At around thirty attendees per presentation, that's sixty people an hour. If the show floor is open from 10:00 a.m. to 5:00 p.m. three days a week, that's approximately 420 people per day, or more than 1,200 during the length of the show.

The more people you can move through your booth, the higher your odds for capturing qualified leads and the more successful your booth appearance.

"Tradeshows feel like marathons. But in fact, they're sprints," Andy emphasized.

What about the size of the booth or the company at the show? Ken Newman believes that there isn't a company that wouldn't benefit from having a good spokesperson.

With Ken's help, we got out the trusty calculator. A 10' x 10' has one hundred square feet. Companies have already spent a significant amount of money for the space rental and the booth. Then they've spent more bringing staffers halfway across the country. Even small companies can have tens of thousands of dollars invested in the show. What's another relatively small investment for a professional presenter who is virtually guaranteed to draw *much* more attention to your booth? When you compare what you're already spending, the cost of a presenter doesn't add significantly to your overall budget.

And having a professional presenter definitely makes you stand out from the crowd.

What about type of product or industry? Are some a more natural fit for a presenter than others?

According to Ken and Andy, companies that are most likely to recognize their need for a professional draw have complex products and large budgets. In the case of complex products, a professional presenter can distill a product's essence down to key features or benefits. Because of this, presenters tend to dominate the floor in cases where products and services benefit from explanation—consumer electronics shows, technical IT shows, and health industry shows.

Having said that, both Ken and Andy agree that presenters have a positive impact, regardless of industry type or booth size.

On the other hand, what about using a company employee as a presenter instead of hiring a pro? Both Andy and Ken are admittedly biased toward hiring a pro. Consider the fact that just because you are an employee or owner of a company, it doesn't mean you're the best company spokesperson.

"In spite of the fact that you know the product, getting up in front of people is an acting job," said Ken. "You have to keep the same level of enthusiasm all day long. Professionals do that better than amateurs and very often do it better than the person who came up with the product in the first place."

A professional presenter has the experience to help you identify goals, work with the number of leads you'd like to generate, and shepherd the number of demos and prizes needed to reach those goals. They'll craft a presentation that is suited to meet those goals.

Art and Science of Lead Generation

Lead generation is a combination of science, art, and a little socializing—much like the rest of life.

Once you've collected the proper information, the next step is to make sure it gets back to the office—in a timely manner, to the right people, without being swept away to a dark hole on the other side of Jupiter.

So many tradeshow marketing plans fall victim to Murphy's Law: If something can go wrong, it will. Which means not only should you have a solid method for capturing the leads, but also a foolproof method for getting them back to the office.

If you're sending them digitally, confirm that they arrived at the office. Make backups off-site. Put a copy on a thumb drive.

If you have paper lead forms and need to send them back to the office, make sure they actually get there. If you're going to overnight them via FedEx or UPS, make copies either by scanning them or taking them to a copy machine.

If you have a smartphone, get an app such as ScannerPro, which allows you to take quick snapshots of documents and create PDFs that can then be uploaded to the cloud using Dropbox or something similar.

If you're carrying them back in person, always keep them on your person. Don't put them in your luggage, which can get lost.

In other words, treat your leads like *money*, like *gold*, like your life and job are on the line. *Never let them out of your sight until you know for sure they are back in the office, in the hands of the team that will follow up on them!*

Four out of five tradeshow leads are never followed up on. Even in this day and age, it's still true. And this is one of the most disturbing statistics about tradeshow marketing.

Eighty percent.

It is troubling that tradeshow exhibitors will spend tens or hundreds of thousands of dollars on a new booth, employ staffers, and pay a pretty penny for the booth space rental, but still not follow up on four out of every five leads.

Amazing.

Don't let it happen to you.

Collect the leads and make sure—double sure, triple sure, quadruple sure—that they actually make it back to the office.

What is a proper follow-up method? Is it e-mailing or calling someone once? Or is it a series of follow-up contacts based on the type of lead? Whether it's putting your leads into a marketing automation system, or making the phone call or sending an e-mail as agreed upon at the show, you should confirm that the proper steps will be taken by the designated people within the agreed-upon time frame.

If you don't have specific answers to at least two-thirds of these questions, it's a pretty good bet that you're missing out. Your sales funnel has a few leaks, and you need to plug those leaks.

So many participants see tradeshow marketing as a *fun*, happy, *chaotic* time that they're just glad to come home with a handful of leads they can hand off to their sales team. Unfortunately, tradeshow marketing is so much more. It's a serious business with a lot of money, time, and energy on the line, and it should be treated as such.

Whether your company is new to tradeshow marketing, or you've been doing it for decades, it behooves you to sit down with all the involved parties and start to makeover your marketing from top to bottom. This will help you to analyze any difficulties you'll be experiencing, as well as come up with strategies to address them and add new wrinkles to your overall plan.

Determine your preshow strategy, your show execution strategy, and your follow-up strategy. Create your plan. Work the plan. Debrief after each show and at the end of the year to determine what you did right, what you did wrong, and what can be improved.

Step Ten Challenge

Below are questions for you and your marketing team:

1. What's your show follow-up plan?
2. What's your lead capture method?
3. How many leads did you bring back to the office from each show last year?
4. Who follows up on the leads, and how are those executed: e-mails? phone calls?
5. How well does your team follow your lead-generation and tracking plan?
6. What might you do to improve the system?
7. Are you gaining at least a 5:1 return on your tradeshow marketing program investment?
8. Are you able to measure the return on investment each year and each event?
9. Have you determined the cost per lead at each event?
10. What's the ratio of leads generated to those who become clients?
11. What happens when people stop by your booth? In other words, do you have an activity or some sort of engagement that takes place?
12. What is your follow-up plan? How do you determine the messaging and frequency of individual follow-ups?
13. Are you able to measure the results of your follow-up?
14. Are the people you follow up with glad to hear from you, or are they looking forward to getting off the phone with you? In other words, what is the value you bring to each encounter so that they're happy to take your calls?

BECOMING THE ZEN MASTER OF STATS AND RECORDS

What records should you keep from your schedule of tradeshow appearances?

Answer: *Everything.*

No, seriously. You'll be glad you did.

Can I end this step now? If you keep track of everything, you've done your job.

But *everything* may mean different things to different people. So the topic probably warrants a closer look.

What records do you keep?

At the outset, you'll want to make lists of the products and services that are promoted at each show, along with notes about the graphics that are used.

Beyond the lists of show manuals, products, booth sizes, booth numbers, and electrical layouts, you'll want a record of your tradeshow booth staff. If you have any feedback from the show debriefings, add those.

Take photos—lots of photos. Take photos of the overall booth, close-ups of each graphic, and close-ups of the way the booth fits together. Photograph everything.

Keep lists of leads. Make copies before they're given to the sales team for follow-up. Keep track of what information each lead wanted and when. List any literature that was given away at the show and what was sent to each lead.

Make notes of how many copies of your sell sheets were printed, how many were left over, and how many samples you handed out and the reactions to them.

Six months from now, when some salesperson wanders into your office and asks whether you know what Beverly from the Zee Company was interested in when she stopped by the show, you can pull up the file and provide the answer.

Next, take screenshots of social media posts sent out from the show floor. Often you'll have engaging responses to those posts. Take screenshots of those responses, too.

If someone on the marketing team wants to know about the graphics used last January at the Fancy Foods Show, pull up the photos from that show and show them.

Here's the thing: If you keep everything and organize it well, you'll have easy access to those bits and pieces over time when there are questions about the shows. The more records you keep, the better off you are.

How to keep the records?

While it's great to keep digital copies of everything, and I encourage that method, keeping paper files can be just as effective. If you don't have a company server where you can store the records for employee access (while keeping a separate file on your computer as backup), a simple three-ring binder will suffice.

As we move into cloud storage for digital documents, the transition might mean investigating in DropBox, Evernote, Google Drive, or similar programs that your staff are familiar with in order to give them easy access to store and find documents.

Recordkeeping for tradeshows is often haphazard. Your task is to design an organized storage system so that anyone in the company can quickly access records.

Why keep so many records?

The purpose is twofold (maybe threefold). First, you want to track trends from year to year and find records showing what you did last time for your electrical layout, drayage costs, and so forth.

The second reason is that the process enables the rest of your team to access records when a question comes up.

"Hey, we're on the tradeshow floor trying to set up the large fabric wall, and for some reason there are no setup instructions!" It was a frantic phone call from three thousand miles away.

No worries, you think. Just pull up the file from the archives and e-mail it within a moment or two and save the day. Or, if your system is really running in top-notch form, the guy on the tradeshow floor can access it from a tablet within seconds of realizing he needs it.

Recordkeeping for tradeshow marketing is often about saving the day, which saves your bacon, which saves your job, which can often make you a hero.

Which brings us to the third reason to keep records: institutional continuity. Chances are, you won't be in your current job until you retire. And even if you are, someone, at some time, will take over your position, and if you leave your successor a thorough record of everything that's been done at the shows for the past several years, your praises will long be sung. You will be remembered as a pretty awesome person. Not only that, your leadership will encourage your successors, likewise, to keep the same kinds of records.

Recordkeeping also brings up the issue of increasing the *knowledge base* of your team. The more your marketing team and booth staff know about the company's tradeshow marketing, the better informed they'll be both on and off the tradeshow floor. And the more successful your tradeshow marketing efforts will likely be.

As tradeshow marketing director, your challenge is to capture and archive everything you can. Organize it in a way that you and your team can easily find specific items.

Want to be ahead of your competitors? Thorough recordkeeping is a way to differentiate your company.

Here's a list of additional items to consider keeping in your archives:

- Number of shows per year
- Specific goals and objectives of each show
- Main benefits of exhibiting at specific shows
- Products (type and count)
- Literature (type and count)
- Graphics (number and dimensions)
- Graphic designer
- Booth number
- Show manual
- Booth size and other details that change from show to show
- Booth space rental cost
- Carpet rental costs
- Cost of new booth
- Cost of rental booth
- In-booth demonstration details
- If doing demos, how many?
- Number of people who show up at each demonstration, on average
- Total number of people who viewed demonstrations

- Travel and lodging costs
- Shipping costs and related information, such as shipper, bill of lading, and so forth
- Drayage costs
- Rental furniture costs
- Number of times at this specific show
- Annual exhibit budget
- Exhibit booth resources (designer/fabricator)
- Booth personnel who attended the show
- Client meetings/entertainment costs
- Type of lead-generation system
- Sales leads generated
- Sales resulting from leads
- Number of leads followed up
- Specific information on what was sent and to whom
- Visitor count
- Samples used during the show
- Notes from staff debriefing
- Comments and questions from visitors
- Photos of booth, visitors, competitors
- List of competitors near you
- Reaction to competitors' new booths, if noted
- Competitors' products being promoted
- Strengths and weaknesses of your company and your competitors
- Show plan for booth staff
- Training for booth staff
- Responsibilities and job descriptions of each staff member
- Booth staff schedules
- Number of business cards taken/handed out

As you can see, many details may be archived. The more things you track from show to show, the more informed you'll be. As information is shared throughout the marketing team and with everyone else involved in the company's tradeshow marketing efforts, the higher the knowledge base of those employees and contractors.

The more well informed your team, the better your chance of success. It all works together, like a crazy waltz, like dancing bears on unicycles.

Sales Return On Investment (ROI) On Tradeshow Marketing

To determine tradeshow ROI, first calculate how much you spent on the show. This includes the cost of your booth, as well as expenses related to client parties, flights, travel, transportation, hotels and accommodations, food, booth staff salaries, show services, and so forth. If, for example, the total you spent on the show is $100,000, that's the number you start with. (It could be argued that booth staff salary should be left out of the calculation because if your company weren't at the show, they'd be in the office where they'd still earn their salary and they'd still be working toward other lead-generation and sales activities. I say it's still worth including in your calculation.)

ROI = (gross profit − $100,000)/$100,000

Your gross profit comes from sales booked directly from event leads. If you hadn't been there, you wouldn't have met those folks, and you wouldn't likely be selling to them as a result. If the resulting gross profit is higher than your total investment, you can point to a positive ROI. The question then becomes: Did we generate enough profit from this show to justify going back in the future?

Once you determine the exact amount spent on the event, you will then determine the leads and sales that were generated as a result of participating in the tradeshow. Whether you use your internal sales tracking, or input all the leads into a tool such as Salesforce, your task is to track the amount of sales generated as a result of the new contacts.

It may be that your product is the type that doesn't realize sales for months, or perhaps years, yet the money will eventually still arrive from sales generated as a result of appearing at particular shows.

It may also be that you have a type of product, like our fictional marketer Katie whose company, Gotcha! Cookies 'n' Treats, offers edibles, where clients will continue to reorder indefinitely.

In such cases, time and effort is needed to calculate the exact ROI. Still, that shouldn't stop you from running some ROI calculations every month and then running a final ROI calculation at year's end to determine that year's final ROI.

In some cases, the lifetime value of a single client can justify the cost of a single tradeshow appearance. You may find that one new distributor more than makes up for the single show investment.

On the other hand, sales results may be less than desired, and you'll have a tougher time calculating a show's ROI. In this case, you and your staff should discuss the numbers and make a decision on whether or not to continue participating in a specific show.

You can also calculate ROI for an entire year by adding the costs of all shows to a single sum, and then calculating the total sales from all the shows. This will give you a general tradeshow marketing ROI from year to year. By calculating each single show, however, you may be able to identify shows that are underperforming, and elect to drop them from your schedule or make modifications for better results. The fact is, if you effectively apply all of the ideas in this book, those underperforming shows should become better performers.

Download a simple Excel spreadsheet where you can input your numbers and determine your ROI. Check the back of the book for the link.

Step Eleven Challenge

- Determine which member(s) of the team are responsible for archiving all the information mentioned in this step.
- Create a system to store the information and make it easy to find when needed.
- Check in on every show and twice a year to make sure all pertinent information is archived and available. A regular audit will be worth the time and effort.

STIRRING THE PUBLIC RELATIONS AND MEDIA POT

Public relations (PR) and media outreach at tradeshows appears to be something that companies want—and would love to have—but they often don't spend a lot of time, effort, or money in an organized attempt to make happen. In other words, a lot of opportunities go unexplored.

However, an organized effort to develop and execute a media plan can pay off in tens or even hundreds of thousands of dollars in earned media. As you probably know, an article in a trade magazine or on an industry website with lots of traffic has more credibility than an ad.

Where does media outreach come from, and how does it work?

Most shows have a "press list" of preregistered media available for exhibitors. By starting with that list, schedule meetings with reporters at the show. Don't think they'll find you on their own. Be proactive and contact them ahead of time to make sure they know they're invited to come by your booth for an interview.

Show organizers often offer items and events such as press media tours, awards opportunities, press conferences, video pitches, show-related online press centers, opportunities for guest blogging, and more. And while the show organizers do make an effort to let all exhibitors know about these, sometimes the opportunities are not readily evident and can easily slip between the cracks.

Keep in mind that most editors and reporters prefer to be contacted via e-mail, so they can read and respond at their convenience. It's also important to develop ongoing relationships with various media outlets covering your industry.

By developing a media contact plan, you can identify the most prominent media outlets. Create a schedule for contacting them. Some outlets will be more desirable than others, depending on the amount of material they generate, how often they publish, and how prominent and recognizable they are.

Once the plan is in place, run the plan. You don't necessarily need a new product. You can let the media know about events, tradeshows, new clients, or a particularly successful experience, such as a new product launch or the biggest year in the company's history.

Your media contacts should also be aware of the names and contact information of your company's spokespersons, such as the CEO, the marketing director, and so on.

Media Kit

Develop a media kit, press kit, or online media center. The intent is to address questions from the media, customers, or investors regarding the company. Even though the names are usually interchangeable, in the end, you'll have material that is essentially a résumé for your company.

Despite your probable desire to throw every bit of information into the press or media kit, it's easy to include too much. Strike a balance between showcasing everything the company has done in the past ten years and including just bare-bones listings of products and company management personnel.

According to Al Lautenslager of Market-for-Profits.com, writing in *Entrepreneur* magazine in 2012, a press kit may include the following:

- Letter of introduction
- Company information
- Product and service information, including a product, service, or performance review
- Recent press publications and articles
- Press releases
- Audio and video files of radio and TV interviews
- Sample news stories
- List of frequently asked questions

Other things that might be included:

- Nonprofit and community service ventures
- Photos
- Recent awards
- White papers
- Event schedules
- Statistics relating to your industry, demographics, and target audiences
- Missions, goals, and objectives
- Downloadable logo art
- Giveaway information
- An order form

Press kits can be printed and mailed as well as made available in folders at the tradeshow or other events. Online media areas may have the usual stuff as well as media-rich content such as interviews with management, video testimonials, demonstrations, and more.

While it might feel appropriate to offer press kits even when people don't ask for them, if their response is cool, don't feel obligated to hand out a bunch of printed material that will be tossed in the garbage can. Instead, you might point them to your online media kit with a link printed on a business card or postcard.

Media Kit and Contact Plan

Katie, our intrepid exhibitor with Gotcha! Cookies 'n' Treats, spent time putting a media kit together in the past year in an attempt to have a more organized outreach program.

"What makes your media kit so critical?" I asked.

"It's something new to the company, so we floundered a bit. But that was OK, because it meant we were doing something. We asked around, we looked at other companies to see what they were doing and got some good intel.

"Having a media kit with critical information in one place is important, we found, but it had to tie in to our overall media outreach program," Katie added. "We assembled a list of media to reach out to. Some we knew, many we didn't. We were looking for new outlets to spread the word about our cookies and treats."

"Did you make use of any preregistered media lists?" I wondered.

"Some shows had them, some didn't," Katie responded. "But that didn't stop us from letting people know about what we are doing. It's easy to update everything online, so that all we had to do was send out a brief capsule story with a link to photos, videos, testimonials, and other information."

"What about other show advertising or media opportunities, like the show manual, website, show app, or other exhibitor resources?"

"We've looked at them, and are considering a few of them for shows next year," she said. "The show organizers have been very helpful. They want everyone to succeed, too, because that helps word of mouth for their show."

"What do you want out of your show media execution plan?" I asked. "Do you have measurable and identifiable goals and objectives? Also, make sure that your objectives are within your reach. Can you actually accomplish them?"

"That's certainly been on my mind, although I don't think I've articulated them precisely, or certainly not as well as I could," said Katie. "But I think we're well on our way! After all, we keep learning and adding, so any movement in the right direction is a positive."

As you set goals, you might want to shoot for more positive media mentions about your products or services. You might have specific objectives, such as a TV interview on a cable news network or a feature article on your new product in a major industry publication. In your media plan preparation, make a list of your objectives.

Objectives will likely include a list of the products presented, your key prospects, any regional areas or characteristics that are important, and the messaging that goes along with those products and goals.

If you want to be featured on a cable news network, what are the odds of that actually happening? You may have a good contact and prior conversation, leading you to believe that it's possible, so it actually might. Or you might be spitting in the wind.

Ditto with magazine cover stories. They are rare; they may not be likely. If that's the case, perhaps you shouldn't spend precious time pursuing them.

Ask yourself if the objective is meaningful. You may say, for example, that you'd like to improve the company's impact in a few key media outlets by 10 or 20 percent over the same quarter of the previous year.

And finally, is it measurable? If you can't measure it, you probably won't be able to achieve it, or know when you have achieved it.

Next, determine your strategy for achieving those goals and objectives.

You've already got the press kit, so that may be part of your strategy, along with meetings at the show, distributing press releases, or submitting products for awards consideration.

Show meetings with press representatives are probably the most critical. Not only will you be able to answer questions in real time, but getting to know the various individuals reporting on the industry will help to develop relationships. Over time, you will develop a good working relationship where you can just pick up the phone and let the reporter know you have something new and you'd like him or her to take a look.

Each show may have more than one objective, so you'll need strategies for each. If you want to increase media mentions and coverage by 35 percent, you may include strategies that include putting out a press kit, giving booth tours, planning media appointments at the show with key interviews, and issuing press releases. Each of these strategies may involve various tactics. For example, conducting booth tours may mean you have to schedule a dozen media reps.

At the end of the show, make a list of all the results from execution of your tradeshow media plan. Create a spreadsheet, showing your objectives, strategies, tactics, and the final results. In reviewing these results with your team and management, you will learn what worked, what didn't work, and how to make adjustments for the next show.

Some companies are small enough that having someone work as tradeshow manager full time is not feasible. In this case, it might make sense to hire an experienced outside agency to do media outreach for you. Often a good, experienced agency has more contacts with the press within your industry and relationships with reporters. It may be more costly than doing it yourself, but if the results are noteworthy and you see more sales as a result, it's probably worth it.

Step Twelve Challenge

Below are questions to ponder and discuss with your team:

1. Do you have a specific plan with measurable, achievable goals for each show?
2. Are you able to execute your plan with the personnel and resources you have available?

3. How many media outlets did you talk with at your last tradeshow?
4. What kinds of coverage did you get at that show?
5. What kinds of coverage do you think is missing and that you could have gotten?
6. Who handles your media outreach? Is it internal, or do you hire an outside agency?
7. What is your plan for contacting media outlets at your next tradeshow appearance?
8. Which media outlets have done articles, profiles, or videos of your company or its products or services in the past?
9. How long ago did those articles appear?
10. How did you use those articles once they were in print or available online?
11. Did you generate revenue or profits from your PR and media objectives? If so, was it measurable?

DO QR CODES STILL KILL KITTENS? AND OTHER TECH QUESTIONS

I t used to be, in the deep past of just a few years ago, that quick response (QR) codes were going to be the next big thing. Then along came reality. Meaning that the reality of how they actually work for most people falls short of both the dream and what your local QR code–promoting agency has to say on the matter.

The fact is, QR codes can work in certain situations. It became apparent, though, that most people weren't scanning them, and when they did, as often as not, the attempt to scan failed. But QR codes hardly took over the digital landscape, simply, perhaps, because the field is moving too fast for any one technology, tactic, or app to take hold.

As time goes on, new technologies will arise and old ones will fail. Your challenge is to see the forest for the trees and use the technologies that work for you. Just because an exhibitor down the aisle is using something doesn't mean it'll work for you.

If you are going to use QR codes, however, follow these guidelines. At least you won't look like an idiot, and you may actually get some good use out of them.

If you want your QR code to function the way it should and provide pertinent information to the person you have scanning it, make sure it's easily accessible and scannable.

- Put the QR code in an easily accessible location; the final size should be at least 3" x 3" to about 12" x 12".
- Put the QR code at eye level.
- Include a call to action, such as "Scan me to win!"
- Optimize the landing page for viewing on a smartphone.
- Test everything before the show.
- Don't assume that everyone has a QR code reader. Either give directions on how to download an app or offer the URL in another form, such as a postcard-size piece of paper.
- Don't include large graphics or videos on your landing page. Make it simple. Lots of data will slow delivery time and frustrate the viewer.
- Confirm that the tradeshow site has good cell coverage.
- Set up your landing page so you can track metrics and analytics.

If you have a good reason to use a QR code and it passes all of the above tests, you can probably get away with using it. Don't expect it to be the end-all and be-all marketing tool. Just expect it to be another arrow in your marketing engagement quiver.

Other Technologies

Earlier in the book, we touched on lead gathering and tracking using a smartphone app. With the current penetration of smartphones into the population, if you're not taking advantage of that technology, you'll be left in the dust because you can bet most of your competitors are.

Besides lead retrieval, technological advances can relate to badge scanning, session tracking, mobile events, audience response, radio-frequency identification (RFID) tracking, and more.

Badges are now scanned at many event and tradeshow stops, and technology can be used to move people from one location to another.

Phone-charging stations are also more common, and if they are well branded, their locations can be good spots to make positive impressions on visitors. A charging station is also an implicit invitation to spend more time in your booth. Depending on your goals, that may or may not be a good thing as some visitors can overstay their welcome.

The costs of LEDs and digital signage continue to drop, which drives up usage. Many exhibitors also use digital picture frames instead of printing a ton of graphics. It is an attractive, low-cost, green option.

If you really want to test your brain, try Googling iBeacon, Apple's new, low-powered location service, or NFC (Near Field Communication). Then refresh your brain by Googling RFID.

The development of smartphone and tablet apps aimed at exhibitors and attendees is growing. App usage ranges from informing attendees and self-promotion to collaboration and communication. Other applications address matchmaking between exhibitors and attendees, allowing visitors to find suitable products and companies based on keyword matching.

A recent report from the ASAE Foundation, Exhibit Industry Foundation, Freeman, Gaylord Entertainment, and the Professional Convention Management Association (PCMA) Education Foundation (there's a mouthful) entitled, "Scenarios for the Future: Convention Exhibits and Tradeshows 2016," examines the future of events and tradeshows, discussing possibilities ranging from likely (the future is now) to slightly absurd (tradeshows will go away and be replaced by…what?). In any event, many aspects will continue to ring true, like the value of lead gathering, creating a unique experience for visitors, and the importance of closely monitoring changes within your industry.

Some of the key takeaways from the paper urge readers to focus on tracking data, staying on digital alert, remaining flexible, delivering something new to audiences, and staying focused on the reasons for being there in the first place.

Without a doubt, technology is driving change, and only a fool would predict anything much beyond the limited horizon. Staying aware of new technologies, apps, software, and materials in your industry is well advised.

Beyond staying up on technology and paying attention to how colleagues and competitors are using the newer apps and gizmos, it's always worth staying abreast of business in general. I spend a lot of time each month perusing the latest issues of publications such as *Inc.*, *Fast Company*, and *Wired* to see what's getting ink. And these magazines have social media feeds and blogs as well, with coverage extending beyond the print editions.

Step Thirteen Challenge

- Discuss the future of your company's tradeshow marketing program in general terms, and imagine what might play out over the next several years. Where do you see it going? What's going to change? What's going to stay the same?
- Are there technologies other exhibitors are using, but you aren't?
- Is there something you think would be a good addition to your booth or exhibiting efforts, but you haven't seen it yet? Make a note—maybe you need to invent it!
- What apps are available from show organizers at your next exhibition?
- Is your current technology meeting your needs?
- If not, what's missing?

If you use QR codes:

- Are instructions posted plainly near all QR codes?
- Do you test every code thoroughly?
- Is the landing page optimized for smartphones?
- What are the results of your QR code usage?
- Are you tracking QR code usage from show to show?

OUT OF THE NEST: YOUR TIME TO FLY!

Remember, way back in the introduction to this book, when I mentioned the concept of increasing the knowledge base of your tradeshow marketing team? It's come up several times throughout, the intent being that if the members of your team know everything about the process, or as much as is possible, as every other member of your team, your success in tradeshow marketing will be greater—much greater.

Think about that for a moment. What if you could take the combined knowledge of your team members and make it available to everyone individually?

Scary, eh? Yes, and it's impossible, too. We're all different. We think differently and we process information differently. What John over in social media knows is different from what your tradeshow manager Julia knows.

However, imagine a world in which John takes time to write down his thoughts and processes at each show and is able to communicate his understanding of what he does and how it impacts the overall program. Imagine if Julia could do the same.

Now apply that possibility to every single member on your team. What if they were trained not only to document what they do, but were also asked hard questions about how the process works and how each step applies to the overall effort?

That would take guts and trust, not to mention more work than they probably are now comfortable with doing.

But hear me out: This is doable. And it is worth it in so many countable and uncountable ways.

If you ask each team member to compile a brief document on what he or she does and to share it with everyone else, suddenly you have everyone seeing things from all eyes, not just individual eyes.

This is how you plant success, by trusting everyone to both observe, document, and share what they do, and take time to understand what all fellow team members do.

It may be that tasks overlap a bit. It may mean that you don't have a lot of additional information to share. I've seen some marketing teams that work together very well, with each member having thorough understandings of other team members' jobs and how they fit into the overall scheme of things. I've seen marketing teams of one or two where each player wears a lot of hats.

But that's not always the case, and I would argue that even if your team thinks it has a good understanding of everyone's tasks, there is still a lot to learn.

Step Fourteen Challenge

Here's your final exercise with your team. If you've been discussing the program with them from the beginning, this final exercise should be a lot of fun and very revealing.

It's time to assess the current state of your tradeshow marketing and to look at your goals for the short, medium, and long term.

No doubt you've already done that throughout the book if you've been reading closely and paying attention to the suggestions and lessons.

Discuss the following items with your team, make notes, and from those notes and assessments, determine by priority what needs to change first, second, and third.

On a scale of one to ten, with ten being excellent and one being so horrible you wouldn't want to tell even your mother, how successful would you judge your tradeshow marketing?

Based on that answer, what would you like to change in the short term, and what changes would you like to make before your next show?

What would you like to change in the next year?

What considerations are deemed important by the company's marketing department, within the next two to five years, regarding your tradeshow marketing endeavors? Is it the size of the booth, market expansion, or other kinds of outreach? Is it developing a different way of having attendees learn about your offerings?

Identify your most important opportunities of improvement.

Now that you've spent time (and probably heartache, if you're like most exhibitors), catalog those opportunities.

It might mean expanding your tradeshow social media engagement, or finding better ways to demo or sample your products.

It may mean a stellar, rock-star booth making you stand out at the show.

Or it may simply mean investing in training for booth staff or upgrading show records so that they're all available digitally, for all parties involved in your marketing efforts.

Every step laid out in this book offers ideas for improvement, such as setting better goals, budgeting, preshow marketing, making sure you're at the right shows, upgrading your booth, and training your staff and bringing them further into the company's communication sphere, as well as tips for interaction strategies for visitors, better social media engagement, content generation for social media, lead generation, recordkeeping, and public relations and media outreach.

Only you know which opportunities are ripe for the picking and which ones are going to take more time, energy, and resources to make happen.

Tradeshow marketing *can be* the best money to spend on marketing. There are hundreds or thousands of companies that continue to prove so, year after year, by investing in tradeshow marketing and seeing fantastic results.

If you're not seeing those results, it's not because tradeshow marketing doesn't work. It *does* work. You just haven't figured out *how* to make it work for *you* yet.

But keep working at it, keep looking for areas of improvement, and you'll continue to make incremental improvements.

And if by some chance you can make wholesale changes and improvements based on the ideas presented in this book, I suspect you'll see some big changes in your results.

So get to it. May your exhibiting always be successful and moving upward!

INDEX

Visit

TradeshowGuyExhibits.com

*Subscribe to Tradeshow Marketing Newsletter
*Download the Tradeshowguy Exhibitor Toolkit
*Download spreadsheets and other tools mentioned
        in this book
*Find your new exhibit - review photo galleries
*Follow TradeshowGuy online

Made in the USA
Charleston, SC
27 October 2015